100
THINGS SUCCESSFUL
PEOPLE DO

100

THINGS SUCCESSFUL
PEOPLE DO

NIGEL CUMBERLAND

First published in Great Britain in 2016 by John Murray Learning. An Hachette UK company.

This edition published in 2017 by John Murray Learning.

British Library Cataloguing in Publication Data: a catalogue record for this title is available from the British Library.

Library of Congress Catalog Card Number: on file.

Hardback ISBN: 978 147 3 63504 3

Paperback ISBN: 978 147 3 63505 0

eBook ISBN: 978 147 3 63506 7

7

The publisher has used its best endeavours to ensure that any website addresses referred to in this book are correct and active at the time of going to press. However, the publisher and the author have no responsibility for the websites and can make no guarantee that a site will remain live or that the content will remain relevant, decent or appropriate.

The publisher has made every effort to mark as such all words which it believes to be trademarks. The publisher should also like to make it clear that the presence of a word in the book, whether marked or unmarked, in no way affects its legal status as a trademark.

Every reasonable effort has been made by the publisher to trace the copyright holders of material in this book. Any errors or omissions should be notified in writing to the publisher, who will endeavour to rectify the situation for any reprints and future editions.

Typeset by Cenveo® Publisher Services.

Printed and bound in Great Britain by Clays Ltd, Elcograf S.p.A.

John Murray Learning policy is to use papers that are natural, renewable and recyclable products and made from wood grown in sustainable forests. The logging and manufacturing processes are expected to conform to the environmental regulations of the country of origin.

John Murray Learning
Carmelite House
50 Victoria Embankment
London EC4Y 0DZ
www.hodder.co.uk

This book is dedicated to my son, Zeb, and to all those working to create a meaningful and unique life filled with successfully accomplished dreams.

'Nobody can build the bridge for you to walk across the river of life, no one but you yourself alone. There are, to be sure, countless paths and bridges and demigods which would carry you across this river; but only at the cost of yourself; you would pawn yourself and lose. There is in the world only one way, on which nobody can go, except you: where does it lead? Do not ask, go along with it.'

– Friedrich Nietzsche

Contents

Foreword by Marshall Goldsmith   xiii

About the author   xv

Introduction   xvii

1 Follow your dreams   2

2 Ask for help   4

3 Create your future   6

4 Be emotionally intelligent   8

5 Do the opposite   10

6 Turn work into play   12

7 Start each day well   14

8 Make friends with your past   16

9 Take breaks   18

10 Be a student of life   20

11 Trust your gut   22

12 Banish your stress   24

13 Be likeable   26

14 Say 'yes'   28

15 Say 'no'   30

16 Volunteer your time   32

17 Focus on things you can control   34

18 Live within your means   36

19	Live in the 'real world'	38
20	Stay focused	40
21	Love more	42
22	Reinvent yourself	44
23	Stay healthy	46
24	Forgive others	48
25	Be part of a tribe	50
26	Exude confidence	52
27	Give credit where it's due	54
28	Reduce attachments to possessions	56
29	Build rapport	58
30	Live mindfully	60
31	Accept compromises	62
32	Be more than your 9–5	64
33	Know yourself	66
34	Embrace the journey of getting older	68
35	Be both an extrovert and an introvert	70
36	Live with an open mind	72
37	Be the best parent	74
38	Walk away from pollution	76
39	Leave your comfort zone	78

40	Appreciate those closest to you	80
41	Seek wisdom and use it	82
42	Model the best	84
43	Have the courage to fail	86
44	Accept yourself	88
45	Watch and manage your thoughts	90
46	Remember people	92
47	Discover what drives you	94
48	Appreciate what you've got	96
49	Make peace with your parents	98
50	Laugh more	100
51	Stay unique	102
52	Sleep well	104
53	Go your own way	106
54	Seek simplicity	108
55	Do it today	110
56	Seek experiences over things	112
57	Have clearly written goals	114
58	Give reading your full attention	116
59	Get a thick skin	118
60	Be generous	120

61	Eat and drink well	122
62	Seek and create harmony	124
63	Get home on time	126
64	Work for as long as you can	128
65	Have great body language	130
66	Choose and keep your friends wisely	132
67	Be curious	134
68	Do what you say	136
69	Pause before you press 'Send'	138
70	Make friends with fear	140
71	Tell the truth	142
72	Become an expert at something	144
73	Apologize when you are wrong	146
74	Stay in touch with old friends	148
75	Keep the bigger picture in mind	150
76	Embrace technology	152
77	Persist and don't give up	154
78	Watch out for addictions	156
79	Spend more time outside in nature	158
80	Use your intelligence wisely	160
81	Focus on character not popularity	162

82	Say goodbye to toxic people	164
83	Learn from your grandparents (before it is too late)	166
84	Have a true character that makes you proud	168
85	Practise gratitude	170
86	Focus on good news	172
87	Genuine success cannot be faked	174
88	Grow old disgracefully	176
89	Breathe well	178
90	Travel far	180
91	Keep a journal	182
92	Get lost ... and find yourself again	184
93	Plan ahead	186
94	Tick off your bucket list	188
95	Help to sustain the planet	190
96	Connect with something bigger than yourself	192
97	Unlearn everything	194
98	Mentor others to success	196
99	Leave a legacy	198
100	Regret nothing	200
	Afterword	202

Foreword by Marshall Goldsmith

We all know the person we *want* to be. Unfortunately, it's not always easy to *be* that person every day of our lives. We're all made up of habits and subject to triggers that shape our behaviour; sometimes they work for us and sometimes against us. Successfully navigating this complex minefield to become the person you aspire to be can be challenging.

Nigel's latest book can help.

It sets out an inspiring and practical code for successful living and working in the twenty-first century. Inside these pages you'll find a powerful reminder of the many ways you can make your life – and other people's lives – more successful – at work, at home, in your relationships, with your health, wealth and in retirement. It will help you identify what success means to you and give you the building blocks for making that success a reality.

Nigel is certified and trained in my *Stakeholder Centered Coaching* process – a feedback-based process that can help anyone achieve their chosen life and work goals. The 100 ideas and activities collected here have been carefully selected and designed to help you do the same.

Just as I point out in my recent book, *Triggers: Creating Behavior That Lasts – Becoming the Person You Want to Be*, the difference between success and failure is as simple – and as hard – as mastering the behavioural triggers that shape us. The insights and actions Nigel proposes here go hand in hand with that message. But reading alone isn't enough. You need to act on them, so I urge you to follow through with the activities and exercises.

At the start of this foreword I said that we all know the person we *want* to be, but *being* that person is hard. This is your chance to overcome whatever obstacles are stopping you.

Read it, act on it and experience the difference.

Marshall Goldsmith Ph.D., best-selling author of *Triggers*

Dr Marshall Goldsmith has been recognized by the American Management Association as one of 50 great thinkers and business leaders who have impacted the field of management over the past 80 years – and by Business Week as one of the most influential practitioners in the history of leadership development. Marshall has been recognized as the number-one 'Leadership Thinker in the World' and among the top five 'Most Influential Business Thinkers in the World', as well as the number-one executive coach at the 2015 biennial Thinkers50 awards ceremony in London.

About the author

Nigel Cumberland is the co-founder of The Silk Road Partnership, a leading global provider of executive coaching and leadership training solutions to some of the world's leading organizations. He has lived and worked in locations as diverse as Hong Kong, Budapest, Santiago, Shanghai and Dubai, experience that has helped teach him what it takes to succeed in life.

Previously, Nigel worked as a multinational finance director with Coats plc as well as for some of the world's leading recruitment firms including Adecco. In addition, he co-created an award-winning recruitment firm based in Hong Kong and China, which he later sold to Hays plc. Educated at Cambridge University, UK, Nigel is an extensively qualified executive coach and leadership training professional. He is the author of a large number of management and leadership books among the most recent of which are: *Secrets of Success at Work: 50 Techniques to Excel* (Hodder & Stoughton, 2014), *Finding and Hiring Talent In a Week* (John Murray Learning, 2016) and *Leading Teams In a Week* (John Murray Learning, 2016).

Nigel is married to an amazing woman named Evelyn who works as a successful artist. He has two wonderful children – a son, Zeb, and a stepdaughter, Yasmine.

Introduction

What does success mean to you? What kind of success would you like in your life?

Success is the accomplishment of any number of possible aims, dreams, aspirations or goals.

It's very personal and unique to you. Your greatest desire could be someone else's idea of hell; you might want to be an award-winning chef while your best friend hates cooking.

To be able to look back and say 'I lived a successful life' means successfully pursuing a myriad of aims and goals.

This book is your guide to accomplishing them, from your largest and most audacious through to the smallest and most mundane.

Think about it now. What does success look like?...

- Getting promoted?
- Flourishing in a new leadership role at work?
- Losing weight?
- Jogging every evening?
- Becoming a published author?
- Retiring in good health?
- Bringing up your children well and seeing them create their own families?
- Being at peace?
- Paying off your mortgage in full?
- Gaining a particular qualification?
- Following your heart without regrets?
- Having wonderful people in your life?
- Learning a foreign language?
- Recovering from a serious illness?
- Saving a particular amount of money?
- Loving your work and never feeling stressed doing it?
- Being happy and content with what you have?

These are just suggestions based on goals I hear from the clients I coach. Take time out now to write down your own list. Don't edit yourself and don't worry about what order the ideas come to you in. Just them flow out in a stream of consciousness.

Your list probably seems pretty endless and one thing is for certain – it will change with each passing day. You may succeed in reaching the summit of one 'mountain' only to have fresh insights about other mountains. Mountains you didn't even know were there. Priorities and dreams change.

The 100 chapters that follow will help you achieve any kind of success you can imagine. The ideas relate to all areas of your work and life:

- work and career
- relationships and parenting
- personality and character
- wealth and finances
- health and peace
- learning and studying
- retirement and legacy.

Every chapter features a new idea that will help you get closer to your goals. The ideas are introduced and explained on the first page, while the second page features exercises and activities, small and large, that you can start doing today to give you the optimal mindset, habits and behaviours you need to maximize your chances of success.

Some of the activities will be new to you; some will seem like common sense. Either way, it's really important that you do them. They are designed to help you form new habits and program your mental software to help you achieve success. Few people do these things in a conscious or deliberate way. Successful people do.

You will discover activities for now and activities for later depending on what's happening in your life right now. If an idea or activity doesn't apply to what's happening to you, set it aside and return to it at a later date.

Who am I to talk about success?

The ideas in this book come from my having spent over 15 years coaching and mentoring people from all walks of life throughout the world. From this wonderful work I have drawn up this list of the 100 most important areas we need to focus on to achieve genuine success in all areas of our lives.

I have practised what I preach and worked hard to achieve some of my goals, allowing any failures and bumps along my road to be my teacher and guide. Before we go on this journey together, it seems only right that I should share some of my journey with you. In my half-century I have:

- been in a wonderful and healthy marriage with two fantastic children, a 16-year-old son and a 24-year-old stepdaughter
- won a place at Cambridge University and rose to become a regional finance director with a FTSE100 company at the age of only 26
- fulfilled a dream of travelling and spent 26 years living in over eight countries
- successfully co-founded and sold a company in a multimillion-dollar deal
- become an established author and speaker
- followed my passion for helping others through my coaching practice, the Silk Road Partnership
- learned to be at peace with how I am and what I have in my life – this is perhaps my most important success.

All that remains is for me to wish you good luck in your own search for success. The ideas and activities you are about to discover will help you live the successful life you deserve.

FOLLOW YOUR DREAMS

'You will live a much better life if you pursue your passions. People who work on the things
that they love usually enjoy life more than everyone else does simply because they are
chasing their dreams.'

Richard Branson

Dreams are the fuel for your success. Without them there can never be any meaningful and lasting success in your life. Like a car engine without high-quality fuel you risk living a life that never quite gets started.

Behind every successful person there is a dream fulfilled. I have coached dozens of successful people and all have come to their success through achieving at least one of their dreams. It may have been a dream from their childhood or a dream that appeared later in their life, but there is always at least one dream linked to their achievements – something that motivated, drove, excited and captivated them. This dream becomes the goal that pushes you to believe in the impossible, to make unexpected life changes, to step out of your comfort zone and to take unimagined risks.

As adults we often choose to ignore or forget what we really love. We let ourselves be driven by other people's guidance and expectations. I can speak from painful experience: at school I loved Geography but followed others' advice and studied Economics at university. I became an accountant rather than following my own career dreams. Have you made a similar choice in your life? Sometimes it is only with hindsight that you realize you were not following your own path.

Successful people never forget what they love to do and are passionate about. They quickly learn to follow their own path and to make the right choices, no matter how crazy or unpopular they might appear to others. Just look at Steve Jobs, founder of Apple, who quit studying at a prestigious university to pursue his dreams.

Behind every successful person there is a dream fulfilled.

Put it into action

Know your own dreams

What is your dream? What do you really want to achieve? What dreams should you be chasing?

Make a list using a mixture of words, doodles and pictures. This can help you see connections between your ideas and discover long-forgotten goals and desires. The following questions will help you:

- As a child what did you love to do and want to become?
- If money was not an issue, what kind of life and work would you choose to have?
- What parts of your life today do you really love and want more of?
- What do you enjoy doing in your spare time?
- Which aspects of your friends' or colleagues' lives do you look upon with a little envy?

Optimistically believe in your dreams

Think about how you will achieve your dreams and observe if your mind starts being fearful and negative. Perhaps your mind says 'I am too old and it is too late to do this', 'Now I am married with a mortgage I cannot make any big changes to my life' or 'My parents will never support my ideas.' Successful people will tell you that there will always be reasons not to do something. You simply have to find the strength and courage to step forward and start.

Create solutions to achieving your dreams

Knowing how you will achieve your dreams can seem daunting and scary. The remaining 99 chapters in this book will provide you with the tools and solutions you need to remove the fear. The key is to recognize where you are now, where you want to be and explore how to close any gap. It is not easy and I encourage you to enlist the help of those closest to you, ideally aligning your dreams with theirs so that together you can aim to achieve some common dreams.

ASK FOR HELP

'Anyone who takes himself too seriously always runs the risk of looking ridiculous; anyone who can consistently laugh at himself does not.'

Václav Havel

Saying 'I don't know' takes guts but it's an immensely positive reaction and a clear sign that you don't take yourself too seriously. Knowing when you *don't* know the answer and being honest about it is one of the greatest skills you can have. If you aim to be perfect, you'll only end up disappointed. When you admit your blind spots, people will flock to support you.

Too many people act is if they know what to do in situations where they're desperately out of their depth. Too many people try to project confidence in what they're doing or saying, when what they really need is help. There's immense pressure, both at home and at work, to act as if you have all the answers.

The secret is to know when to say: 'Wait a minute – I have absolutely no idea.'

When events challenge you it's tempting to fight back and hold firm to what you once said or believed, leaving you blind to other people's opinions and suggestions. Successful people are happy to admit that they were wrong or that they just don't know.

Life is unpredictable and uncertain. You can never be right all the time. Sometimes the best thing to do is to chill, step back, admit you could do with some help and stop taking yourself so seriously.

> If you aim to be perfect, you'll only end up disappointed.

Put it into action

Find your blind spots

Think about the following question:

Have you ever stubbornly held on to a view or opinion, refusing to explore if you might actually have been wrong?

What were you blind to and why was that so? Can you see a pattern emerging of how you act? Do you always like to win arguments with your partner? Do you never take into consideration what younger people say to you? Have you always hated losing and live with a 'win at all costs' mindset?

Be willing to change behaviours and become more open-minded. Over the course of a typical day making decisions, forming opinions, giving answers, practise asking yourself 'Am I missing anything? Is there a side to this that I am not seeing?'

You need a jester

Uncovering blind spots can be difficult. Enlist the help of family, friends or colleagues to be your jesters. Just as in a medieval king's court, they can tell you when you are being too stubborn, making a fool of yourself or taking yourself too seriously. Which would you prefer: to be told by a jester that you have made a mistake or to be laughed at by others?

Learn to laugh at yourself

Successful people are normally very good at making light of themselves, their mistakes and incorrect thinking. Be ready to happily eat humble pie and always laugh at yourself.

CREATE YOUR FUTURE

'The future is not something we enter. The future is something we create.'

Leonard I. Sweet

Successful people never rely upon chance or fate. You might look at someone successful and think they got lucky – a case of being in the right place at the right time perhaps? The truth is, every piece of good fortune is the result of hours, or even years, of hard work and preparation.

It is not enough simply to have dreams and a plan of how to achieve them. Putting a plan into action involves telling yourself that you will create your own future; that luck or fate will not solely determine what happens. You need the right mindset and you need to take control. Be ready to persist, work hard, sacrifice, and take risks, and to simply do what it takes.

Never resign yourself to what the future holds. I coach too many individuals who have given up on trying to influence their future. They have abdicated responsibility, giving all kinds of lame excuses, blaming bad luck or other people for their lives to date and what the future holds. It is too easy and simplistic to feel that, if you have not succeeded yet, you will not succeed in the future. Overcoming fatalistic thinking is essential if you really want a great future.

Many successful people have had to overcome adversity to achieve their goals – think of Winston Churchill who failed in his political career over many years before eventually becoming the UK's Prime Minister.

Not allowing what happened in the past to determine your future starts in your mind. What you think and feel is key. Are you able to say and believe that you are creating your own future or, to paraphrase the William Ernest Henley poem 'Invictus', that you are the master of your fate?

…every piece of good fortune is the result of hours, or even years, of hard work and preparation.

Put it into action

Do not let others bring you down

You may be keen to share your dreams with your family, friends and colleagues, but do so with care. Too many people take a 'glass half empty' view of life. They may be cynical, jealous, negative or sarcastic. People I coach have shared their goals with loved ones only to be told: 'You must be joking' or 'Get your feet back on the ground.' People may not understand your plans at first, so give them time to come around.

Seek supportive environments in which you can create your future. This might entail pulling away from certain people who are unable to accept and be positive about your plans.

Reframe your view

Are you are having difficulty believing that you can create a fantastic future for yourself? Limiting beliefs can be hard to overcome but it's easier if you understand where they come from. Today, note down all the negatives that are stopping you. It is perfectly normal to fear the worst, to think things are harder than they are. Once you've captured all the limiting beliefs, attempt to reframe your thinking by looking for the positives in negative situations. For example, if you have been fired from a job, recognize that this has given you the freedom to seek new opportunities.

Take a good look at your future plans and dreams and ask yourself what you are most concerned about. Think about the worst that can happen and ask yourself whether that outcome is really likely to occur. Is it a reason to stop you creating the future you desire?

BE EMOTIONALLY INTELLIGENT

'Life is 10 percent what happens to you and 90 percent how you react to it.'

Charles R. Swindoll

Have you been guilty of reacting without thinking, getting angry too quickly, acting jealously or being too easily provoked? Losing control of your emotions can damage your chances of living a successful life. It can easily be the difference between success and failure.

Examples of poor emotional intelligence (EQ) are all around us – people arguing on the bus, parents shouting at their children on the street or someone swearing at their boss while angrily handing in their resignation.

EQ is an essential ingredient of a balanced and fulfilled life. It is the foundation for being a successful partner, parent and work colleague. Successful careers, marriages, families and business partnerships are destroyed by moments of emotional madness.

It's easy to laugh at someone like celebrity chef Gordon Ramsay who swears and shouts in his kitchen, but to ensure a successful life you must avoid making others sad, unhappy or fearful. To do this, you have to learn to keep your emotions in check. If you need to get upset or angry with someone, do so in a very conscious way so that you don't lose control or react without thinking. You cannot spend your life apologizing for having lost control of your emotions.

Being able to put yourself in other people's shoes and see life through someone else's eyes is a sign of high EQ and empathy. Highly empathic people rarely lose self-control, making them better equipped to deal with what life throws at them.

EQ is an essential ingredient of a balanced and fulfilled life.

Put it into action

Pause before reacting

Avoid operating on autopilot and immediately reacting in a way you might regret. This involves being honest with yourself about what you are feeling in that moment, be it jealousy, hurt or anger. In such moments take time out before giving a verbal or non-verbal reaction. Do not speak for a few seconds and sit down if you are standing. People are always calmer and more composed when sitting. If those around you expect you to say something, buy time by saying 'Just give me a moment to think about this.'

Tiredness, overwork or stress cause you to react emotionally. I always advise those I coach to sleep on things and respond the following day. If you need to write a difficult email to someone, it is always better to wait 24 hours after you've drafted the wording before you send it, giving you time to reflect on it and reread it.

Be highly empathic

Recognizing how others are feeling and what they are trying to communicate is a fantastic skill to have. The most memorable bosses have this skill and they are loved for it. Which role models can you turn to for inspiration?

True empathy is not about waiting to understand another person; it is about proactively seeking to do so. It takes effort to give another person your full time and attention; to ask others how they are feeling and if they coping well with things. And don't overlook those closest to you. Never take anyone for granted. Avoid being too preoccupied to sit down and talk with your children, partners and colleagues.

DO THE OPPOSITE

'Look at what the majority of people are doing, and do the exact opposite, and you'll probably never go wrong for as long as you live.'

Earl Nightingale

Unless you think that the majority of people are living successful lives, chances are that at some point you will have to act differently from those around you. Success can take many forms and it is often about standing out from the crowd or being above average, spotting when the crowd moves one way and making sure that you move the other.

Thinking and doing the opposite of what the majority is doing isn't about being different for the sake of being different. There are lots of times when the well-trodden path is the right one to take. Your challenge is to know when it will be in your interest to do the opposite:

- Your friends might talk about studying more but not act; you could commit to completing that much-desired part-time degree course.
- When prices fall, people may panic and sell their shares or houses; you could buck the trend and hold on to them.
- Few people exercise regularly enough and eat healthily; you can be the one who walks to work, goes to the gym and eats healthy food.
- Many people only talk about quitting their jobs to follow dreams of self-employment; you could be the one to break out on your own if your own dreams point this way.

Doing the opposite might make you feel uncomfortable. It can be scary and make you feel lonely and exposed. It is never easy to be seen as going against the grain and ignoring the advice of your colleagues, friends or family, but if you are prepared to explain what you are doing and why, they will come round.

> Success can take many forms and it is often about standing out from the crowd or being above average...

Put it into action

It is OK to act alone

Get used to being uncomfortable and being the odd one out. You really do not need to justify your decisions. Others might question your logic or even sanity – just let them. I gave up a lucrative career in finance to be self-employed. When I did this, many people thought that I was mad or that I was having a breakdown. It hurt me at the time but it didn't change my resolve to become my own boss.

Practise acting the opposite

In what parts of your life are you not achieving your desired results and goals? Are you doing the same things over and over again and getting the same results? Think about what you might do differently to get a better outcome. Here are some mini-case studies to start you thinking:

- Each year at work you try to get noticed in the hope of being promoted. After three years you have not been offered any promotion. Do the opposite – stop trying so hard. Have an honest conversation with your boss to understand why you are missing out. Perhaps better opportunities await you elsewhere and you will need to resign and move on.
- You want to save more money but find by each month's end that you have very little cash left. Do the opposite – rather than trying to save what is left at the month's end, put aside money as soon as you receive your salary. Place it in a fixed-deposit account that you cannot withdraw from and live on the remainder of your salary.
- You want to meet someone new but don't like organized blind dates. Do the opposite – take up more sports and social activities and meet people in a more unplanned way.

TURN WORK INTO PLAY

'There comes a time when you ought to start doing what you want. Take a job that you love.
You will jump out of bed in the morning. I think you are out of your mind if you keep taking
jobs that you don't like because you think it will look good on your résumé.'

Warren Buffet

Do you enjoy your work? Are you happy to get out of bed each morning and dress for the office? If you answered 'no' to either of these questions, you are not alone. In a 2014 Conference Board survey, 52 per cent of Americans claimed to be unhappy at work and in a recent CIPD study 23 per cent of Britons claimed to be looking for a new job. In the same survey only about one-third claim to feel engaged with their work. You can see the effects of this in absence, stress and depression. In fact, you can see it in the rush hour in the tired-and sad-looking faces of so many commuters.

This would not be a problem if work took up only a very small part of your life but unfortunately it consumes most of our daylight hours – typically 2,250 hours per year of your time, assuming a conventional nine-hour working day, five days a week. That ignores your commuting time, overtime and time spent reading all those work-related emails while getting ready for bed.

The majority of people I coach are unhappy or dissatisfied with their working lives. They describe their work in so many depressing ways – as 'boring', 'tedious', 'mind-numbing', 'stressful', 'painful' or even 'scary'. I hear similar opinions as I travel the world from all types of people no matter what their background, education or choice of career.

Unless you have retired or inherited a fortune, you need to work to fund your life. You owe it to yourself to ensure that your working day can be as positive and enjoyable as possible – so much fun that it does not feel like work anymore.

> You owe it to yourself to ensure that your working day can be as positive and enjoyable as possible…

Put it into action

Make your job more enjoyable

Try to do more of what you enjoy and love during your working day. How could you delegate those parts of your job that you do not like? Ask if you could brainstorm with your boss how your job could be changed in some way to make it more engaging and enjoyable. No boss should want their staff to be demotivated and depressed when at work.

If you are unable to change many aspects of your work, you must alter your mindset – learning to stop thinking about your work as boring or dull; viewing the glass as half full rather than half empty; finding the positives in your daily work and career.

Make your workplace more fun

How could you make your working environment lighter, more enjoyable and fun? Talk to friends and visit their offices. Copy great things you see in their workplaces. I have spent time in dozens of different offices. Some stand out as being fun and enjoyable to be in, places where:

- people are laughing, sharing stories and playing music
- there are areas to relax with coffee shops and games
- people seem very positive, kind and civil with one another.

Your work might be dull and tedious but working in such an environment can really lift you up.

Move on

Seriously consider resigning and moving on if you are not able to make your work enjoyable in a great working environment. Find more ideal work in a workplace that you will love and enjoy being in. Life is too short to stay in a job that makes you depressed or unhappy.

START EACH DAY WELL

'Smile in the mirror. Do that every morning and you'll start to see a big difference in your life.'

Yoko Ono

Start each day badly and you wave success goodbye. How you start anything plays a key part in how successful you will be. This is true for how you begin each day. Everyone knows the adage about 'getting out of bed on the wrong side' – it may not be literally true but metaphorically it is 100-per-cent correct.

When you do anything in life there are always reasons why you might not succeed. It is Aristotle who is credited with saying 'well done is half done'. Making a good start goes a long way in helping someone accomplish a task, whether that's a piece of office work, cooking a dish or playing a sport. It's a form of momentum – like giving a stalled car a really good push to get its engine started.

It's much the same with how you start your day. You can always make excuses for not being 100 per cent – you just get the morning blues; you didn't get enough sleep; the bus broke down and you had to walk to work in the rain. The danger comes when it becomes a habit – when you start being OK with starting each day badly. Why rely on having to play catch-up during the rest of the day?

This applies to weekend mornings, too. Are you also starting them positively and optimally, whether you are doing chores or having some precious 'me time'.

Start each day badly and you wave success goodbye.

Put it into action

Adopt some excellent morning habits

- Get up at least 30 minutes earlier than you normally do, enabling you to start your day more calmly without being in your normal rush. Spend a few minutes meditating to some calm music or doing some yoga stretches.
- Make time to sit and have some breakfast. You have been fasting all night and you need to energize your body. If you live with others, eat breakfast together. Be kind and help their day start on a positive note. Smile, make eye contact and ask how they are. Avoid bringing up any negative conversations such as an argument you may have had with them the day before.
- No matter whether you walk, drive, cycle or take the bus or train, decide that you will have a relaxing and stress-free commute to work. Spend this time in ways that make you feel good – by listening to music, reading a book or even sleeping!
- Arrive at work early and ready to go, spending time greeting people and making small talk. Plan your day's to-do list, deciding how you will use different parts of your working day. Do not forget to have your needed cup of coffee.
- Finally, take extra care if you are not a morning person. Make an effort to always act positive and happy both with your family and with your colleagues in the office.

MAKE FRIENDS WITH YOUR PAST

'Some of us think holding on makes us strong; but sometimes it is letting go.'
Hermann Hesse

You cannot change your past, only the way you think and feel about it. When you look back, is there anything you remember that troubles or upsets you? Do you regret missed opportunities, failed relationships or people that you hurt? Do you feel guilt over things you did wrong and poor decisions made, or anxiety over what people did or said to you?

You are not alone. We all carry these thoughts and feelings with us. How might they be affecting you today? Are they holding you back from success in some aspects of your life? Are you scared to commit or to take risks or worried about repeating past mistakes?

You might say 'No, I am fine and I feel none of these things.' You might feel OK and think your past is not haunting you at all. But be aware that at a sub- or unconscious level you may still have these feelings. In all my years of coaching people no one has come to me totally at peace with their past.

Be careful that your memory is not biased – recalling the negatives and forgetting the positives of past events. It is easy to think that you were hurt or upset in the past when in truth you might have only partially understood or remembered what actually occurred – for example:

- feeling neglected when your parents were simply wanting to give you space to make your own choices
- feeling guilty that you resigned from your first job because you didn't want to face your boss's criticisms when in reality that boss might have been a bully whom no one could work for.

You cannot change your past, only the way you think and feel about it.

Put it into action

Take your head out of the sand

Be willing to explore and talk about issues from your past. Do not pretend that everything is fine when it is not. I had a friend who, following a divorce, had not seen his children for over 20 years. I could see how this had affected him, how he had become cynical and harsh about life. He pretended otherwise, saying, 'If my kids don't want to see me, that's OK.' Over time he finally opened up to me about his true feelings of loss and hurt. He has since reconnected with his children.

Understand what really happened

Do you have moments or events in your past that you are not sure about? Try to find out what really happened. Speak to family and friends. If needed, undergo hypnosis or other forms of therapy. Hopefully, what you discover will be better than you might have feared. No matter whether it is or not, you cannot move on from something that you do not truly understand.

Resolve things

To bring you peace there may be events from your past that need resolving. Things you wish to talk about with people from your past. You might be facing something as tragic as having suffered abuse. This will take courage to deal with, particularly if those from your past deny any wrongdoing. Persist – it is very healthy and cathartic to clear the air and to address things that trouble you.

Let the past help you move forward

What wisdom and lessons from your past experiences can help you today? Perhaps you can see patterns in your behaviour. Have you been running away from commitments? Do you avoid speaking up? Do you always attract people into your life who will control you?

TAKE BREAKS

'Each person deserves a day away in which no problems are confronted, no solutions searched for. Each of us needs to withdraw from the cares which will not withdraw from us.'

Maya Angelou

Are you one of the 50 per cent of people in the UK who do not take all of your paid annual leave? This statistic comes from a 2014 Harris Poll that also revealed that 45 per cent of Britons do office work on holiday. Is it any surprise that we see increases in work-related stress, fatigue and burnout? If you fail to take enough breaks, you risk seeing your career break up. In my late twenties I was a finance director based in Hong Kong. I had to work long hours every day for a period of months. There was no time for any breaks or holidays. Stress and burnout hit me and I decided I needed to resign. Metaphorically, I was running on a treadmill at high speed for hours and then fell off.

During your typical working day how often do you stop and take a break, step away from your desk to recharge? Too few breaks can kill your productivity. The business author Stephen Covey explains it well using logging as an analogy – when you are trying to saw a tree down you must take breaks to sharpen your saw. Being a workaholic and failing to do so will leave you blunt and useless.

Even as I write this book I am aware of how productivity declines when you work without a rest. When I feel my concentration disappearing I take a quick break so that I can return energized and focus on my writing.

Taking longer holidays helps you refocus on what is important and reflect on what you want to do with your time. When you break away from your normal environment and daily routines you get new insights into what you do and what you want to be doing.

Too few breaks can kill your productivity.

Put it into action

Take small breaks throughout the day

Take five-minute breaks every 25 minutes. Every two hours take a longer break. Such regular short breaks from your housework or office tasks keep you sharp, awake and focused. This is called the Pomodoro Technique, a time-management tool created by the Italian Francisco Cirillo that has been shown to reduce mental fatigue. Why not share this idea with your work colleagues? Together you can avoid sitting too long in meetings or in front of your computer screens.

When on holiday be on holiday

Take all the days of annual leave that you are entitled to. Split them up into short breaks if you must. Do whatever it takes to take them all. Life is too short not to take advantage of days away from your work. Plan ahead, delegate well and do not feel that you are indispensable at work. I coach too many people who feel guilty in taking their holiday entitlements or in taking any holiday time at all.

When on holiday do not check your work emails. Turn your work phone off. If needed, agree to check your phone for important voicemails and messages only once a day. Does your employer support you in such 'switching off' when on leave? If there is an issue in this regard, talk with your boss and try to reach an understanding. Have the courage to create your own rules for how you will work, if at all, when on holiday.

Treat your weekends in the same way

They are two days of holiday a week. Set rules – for example, that you check your phone and emails only once or twice at most over a weekend. Otherwise, how can you hope to return to work fresh and full of energy on Monday morning?

BE A STUDENT OF LIFE

'The illiterate of the 21st century will not be those who cannot read and write, but those who cannot learn, unlearn, and relearn.'

Alvin Toffler

'Once you stop learning, you start dying.' I first heard this maxim by Albert Einstein in my twenties. At the time I thought it was nonsense. How wrong I was. Learning and success are totally interlinked. Do not make the mistake of thinking that learning ends when you complete your final exams. I thought this. After completing university I proudly told my grandmother that I had finally finished studying. She laughed and told me that you never stop learning because life is constantly teaching you things.

Learning is not simply a task or activity. It is a mindset – a mindset of listening, exploring and being open. It's about being willing, too, to let go of what you thought important or true yesterday. In what areas of your life would you benefit from having a learning mindset? Is it the way you control your finances, bring up your children, keep fit or manage your boss?

Thankfully, life *is* a university. Everything that you do or experience can teach you something, triggering inside you new thoughts, insights and realizations. You might be inclined to forget or ignore experiences that did not go well. Don't. Learning from your mistakes and things that cause you pain is invaluable. The greatest lessons can come from the lowest moments in your life.

Learning new things is in itself a form of success – a process of broadening and deepening your knowledge and wisdom. Try to treat tedious, easy or boring tasks as opportunities to learn something new. Do not switch off and work on autopilot just because the work is easy or monotonous, or because you have done it so many times before.

'Once you stop learning, you start dying.'

Put it into action

What do you need to learn afresh?

You live in a world of constantly evolving knowledge and information. Relevant and useful one day, out-dated the next. You are surrounded by the need to learn about new things – new updates, new processes, new ways of thinking and new products. How well do you keep abreast and up to date?

You also need to be ready to learn to have new ideas and opinions – opinions about people including yourself. It is easier to read a manual about how to use a new TV than it is to up-date your opinions about a work colleague. You might enjoy keeping your mind sharp while stubbornly holding on to some out-dated views of life or of those around you.

What did you learn today?

At the end of each day ask yourself, 'What did I learn today? How does this help me become more successful?' Sometimes the answers may seem obvious. At other times you may have no idea. By starting a daily process of asking these questions you will begin to gain more insights and understanding. Keep a written journal of your answers.

You will have days when something does not go as planned. Spend extra time exploring what you can learn from such moments and events.

What might you need to learn at a more formal level?

To help you achieve your goals, what types of formal learning and training do you need? Would it help your career to gain an accountancy or interior design qualification? Would gaining a teaching or nutrition certification help you to achieve your career dreams? Do you love to cook but have yet to attend any cooking classes? Or are you simply in need of French classes to make your next holiday in Provence more fun?

TRUST YOUR GUT

Gut feeling is your secret weapon for success. How often do you actually listen to it? Gut instinct is when...

- you weigh up some options and one feels best
- you need to choose something and the preferred choice does not feel right
- you try to make a decision and one plan of action feels wrong
- someone makes you feel uncomfortable and nervous
- a situation you are in feels dangerous and you want to leave
- you sense that something you are doing is not going well
- you sense that someone is in trouble and you go to see them
- you have a hunch that your new boss will be great to work under.

Do you ever consciously try to sense your gut feeling by asking yourself, 'What do I feel about this person, situation or decision?' Trusting your gut can help you in the workplace and beyond. The danger is when you let external noise drown out what it's telling you, letting other people's views and opinions take priority over your own.

Have the confidence to listen to your gut. Successful people know when to use different tools and skills and when to follow their intuition. Bill Gates speaks about relying on intuition. When making decisions and facing choices, take into account the available facts and information but listen to what your gut is telling you, too. The well-known journalist Malcolm Gladwell describes this as using and balancing your instinctive and deliberate thinking styles.

Gut feeling is your secret weapon for success.

Put it into action

Overcome your doubts

You might find the idea of listening to your gut feelings odd or even ridiculous. Some people I coach, normally left-brain individuals who use logic and facts all day like engineers or accountants, are not used to following their intuition and feelings. Instead of asking themselves 'What do I feel?', they are more comfortable asking 'What do the facts tell me?'

To become more open to working with your gut feelings, think about a time when

- you had to guess what to do and it turned out to be a good decision
- you ignored a hunch and went with another option, only to find out later that your intuition was right all along.

You do not need to give up being logical, deliberate and fact-driven. Use both types of thinking – your deliberate fact-driven thinking along with a more feeling-focused instinctive thinking.

Be still and listen to yourself

The most powerful way of being able to listen to your own intuition is by being silent. Find a quiet space, slow down and calm your mind. Your goal is to eliminate all that noise going through your head – all those thoughts that appear from nowhere.

Attending meditation classes is a good way to start. A meditation teacher will guide you in the process. Later, when you are comfortable with mediating, you can do it alone or with a partner in your own home.

BANISH YOUR STRESS

'Stress is the trash of modern life – we all generate it but if you don't dispose of it properly, it will pile up and overtake your life.'

Terri Guillemets

Stress can destroy your life. Stress ruthlessly puts out your dreams and robs you of your happiness. It can destroy your health, lead to tensions at home and ruin your career plans. It strikes when you are not at peace or uncomfortable with aspects of your life – and pretty much anything can bring it on:

- The pressure from your boss overwhelms you.
- The commute to and from work makes you tense.
- Your spouse's demands and requests drain you.
- Long hours in the office are making you depressed.
- Your career choice was wrong and makes you feel depressed.
- You have no time alone to focus on yourself.
- You worry about your children's educational success or heath.

Sometimes you will know exactly what is bringing you down or draining you. Sometimes you might not realize anything is wrong until you start feeling stress in your body. Stress is very personal but, regardless of the cause, the symptoms are always the same. Have you ever experienced any of the following?

- lack of energy
- low appetite
- backache
- insomnia
- blurred vision
- headaches

- depression
- tiredness
- irritability
- anger
- listlessness or lack of desire to do anything

My father always used to tell me, 'In a year's time you will have forgotten why you were stressed today, so why stress about it?' Sadly, most of us get stressed regardless. The question is: what can you do about it?

Stress ruthlessly puts out your dreams and robs you of your happiness.

12

Put it into action

Manage the effects before they become chronic

Stress can impact all areas of your wellbeing and health:

- It normally shows itself in your physical health, in symptoms that are easy to spot. Does your body do a good job of showing you that you are stressed through signs such as tight muscles, back aches, blurred eyesight, tiredness and dizziness?
- You may become emotionally stressed. Do you become angry, cold or irritable with those closest to you?
- You may become mentally stressed. Danger signs are feeling drained, burnt out, and tired, or unable to concentrate or think clearly.
- You might become spiritually stressed. Work stress might lead you to question what is important and what you want to do with your life.

Once you are aware of how stress is affecting you, it is easier to make yourself better. Where there's a will there's a way. There are many options depending on how stress is affecting you but the effects can be reduced in simple practical ways such as getting more sleep, exercising, having a massage, practising meditation, relaxing more, taking a holiday, eating healthily or visiting a chiropractor. However, these activities alone are only going to be a temporary stopgap measure. You must be ready to deal with the real causes of your stress.

Tackle the root causes

Your overall aim must be to try to live a stress-free life. This can involve making some difficult choices such as spending less time and energy with certain people or in particular situations. It might involve resigning from a very stress-filled job or walking away from an abusive relationship. The advice throughout this book can help you make the changes you need in your life to make the stress go away.

BE LIKEABLE

'If we want users to like our software, we should design it to behave like a likeable person.'
Alan Cooper

A truly successful life is one filled with friends so it helps if people like being around you. If you suspect they don't, have a think about how strongly you exhibit 'likeable' qualities such as listening well, being trustworthy, kind, generous, compassionate, fun, positive and unselfish. The good news is that you can learn such qualities even if they don't come naturally to you.

Of course, lots of people are successful without being liked. You can probably think of some hugely successful people – people you admire greatly – whom nonetheless you would personally avoid connecting with. This seems like a pretty lonely sort of success.

Try to be likeable but stay true to your self. There will be times when you have to do or say something at the expense of being popular. If you've built up enough goodwill, you'll get away with it. People understand that difficult decisions have to be made and, if you've paid enough into your 'likeability deposit', they will hate the decision but not the person making it. It's like giving a close friend honest but critical feedback – it's not an easy thing to do, but you might be better liked and admired as a result.

The alternative is being likeable but not respected, but no one ever got successful that way.

A truly successful life is one filled with friends…

13

Put it into action

What qualities do you need to develop?

How can you make yourself more likeable? What habits and behaviours are holding you back?

- Have you become more stubborn as you age?
- Do you forget to truly listen to those in your home or office?
- Do you always want to have your way?

Ask one or two friends or family members the following question: 'How could I make myself more approachable and likeable?' Be ready for some replies that might shock and upset you. It might be difficult but they are replies you need to hear and work upon.

Being liked takes sacrifice

There may be moments in your life when you have to choose between 'being liked' and what you really want to do. Imagine your future spouse is a vegan and does not enjoy being with people who eat meat. Could you imagine putting aside your beliefs and feelings, to show support, love and understanding for your partner's?

Be comfortable showing 'tough love'

You cannot always say and do likeable things. There are many times in a relationship that you will get upset, angry or disagree. Parents know only too well the meaning of 'tough love'. In what ways could you start showing 'tough love' with others in your life? Have you been holding back for fear of not being seen as Mr Nice Guy?

SAY 'YES'

> 'Find a way to say yes to things… saying yes means that you will do something new, meet
> someone new, and make a difference. Yes lets you stand out in a crowd, be the optimist, see
> the glass full, be the one everyone comes to. Yes is what keeps us all young.'
>
> Eric Schmidt

Successful people are the ones who say 'yes' when others say 'no'. What would you say if you were offered a job promotion overseas? Would you go for it? What would you say if your partner suggested a new holiday destination, say, Greenland. Would you give it a try?

I'm not suggesting that you jump at everything, ignoring risk, reality and common sense. It is about recognizing those moments when you would typically hold back rather than just going for it.

Lame excuses need to become a thing of the past. You know the kind of thing:

- 'Sorry, I am too busy for that.'
- 'I would but … maybe later.'
- 'I have never done that before.'
- 'Looks exciting but I am OK with what I have.'
- 'I have already decided.'
- 'It is a bit late to do that now.'

Behind these words lie hesitancy, fear, procrastination and aversion to risk. These are not the qualities of someone wanting to succeed in life.

Have you never kicked yourself for turning an opportunity down? If only at the time you had the benefit of hindsight. What would it take for you to have the confidence to say 'yes'? The computer scientist Randy Pausch put it so well: 'It's not the things we do in life that we regret … it is the things we do not.' Start being the one person in the room who says 'yes' when the majority say 'maybe', 'not sure', 'perhaps', 'let's see'…

Successful people are the ones who say 'yes' when others say 'no'.

14

Put it into action

The 'Will I wish I said "yes"?' test

We all have regrets and most regrets are fine. But some are not – not if they make you unhappy, depressed and unable to move on. When coaching leaders facing important decisions and choices, I like to pose them two questions – questions that you should reflect on every time you are faced with an important opportunity or choice:

- Isn't saying 'yes' what you really want to say and do?
- Will you regret it later if you say 'no' today?

What types of big decisions do you foresee having to face in the near future? Will it be about whether you accept a career promotion, sell your house, ask your partner to marry you or hire someone as your successor at work?

How can you get to a 'yes'?

What is holding you back? What do you need to do or know to be able to say 'yes'? Do you need to speak with someone? Does something need to happen? Often, you simply need time, some extra information and the chance to speak with someone about the choices facing you.

What is the worst that can happen?

To help you feel more comfortable about saying 'yes', ask yourself 'What is the worst that can happen? What do I have to lose compared to what I potentially have to gain?'

You will be surprised how often you overdramatize the potential downsides and negatives of your choices. This is particularly true when those choices are new and unknown. It is even more challenging when you are facing a decision that you have never faced before or when you are flying in the face of popular opinion.

SAY 'NO'

'When you say "yes" to others, make sure you're not saying 'no' to yourself.'
Paulo Coelho

OK, so saying 'yes' is great – but saying 'yes' where you mean 'no' will never be a winner for you.

It's easy to get into a pattern of always giving in to daily choices such as where to go or what to eat, but if your voice is never heard you risk becoming subservient to those around you. Having an opinion and exerting some influence even about small things is good. Being a doormat is not a healthy way to live and cannot be good for your self-esteem and confidence.

Saying 'yes' to major life decisions when inside you are crying out to say 'no' is more serious. Doing the opposite of what you feel is right can destroy your chances of achieving your dreams and goals. I have coached too many people who regret going with the flow on major life decisions and now need help living with the consequences.

The choice is yours. As much as you might want to be loved and thanked, you can't please everyone in your life all the time without causing one person to suffer – you.

...saying 'yes' is great – but saying 'yes' where you mean 'no' will never be a winner for you.

15

Put it into action

Tilt the scales back in your favour

You need to recognize and accept that you can only please some of the people some of the time. Other people's needs are important, but so are yours. Your task is to commit to start more regularly pushing back when asked to do something that you really do not want to do whether with your boss and colleagues or your partner. Putting your own needs aside so that you can comply with other people's requests might make you the perfect person to have around, but how long can you play the sidekick role for before something gives?

Enough is enough

Push back diplomatically and kindly.

No need to simply shout 'no'. Instead, seek to be understood and also to appear understanding. When your line manager asks you to stay late to finish work for the third time in a week, push back. Explain that you can and do stay late sometimes but having already stayed late twice that week you need to catch up on your personal life. Apply this same decisiveness and clarity to all requests.

A good line to use in many situations is to say, 'I've agreed to your idea the last few times, now I would like to suggest where we go for dinner / on holiday / what colour we paint the walls.'

VOLUNTEER YOUR TIME

'Be of service. Whether you make yourself available to a friend or co-worker, or you make time every month to do volunteer work, there is nothing that harvests more of a feeling of empowerment than being of service to someone in need.'

Gillian Anderson

Real success is about helping other people succeed. To be well educated in a society of increasing illiteracy is not real success; neither is to be well fed and healthy while millions die of malnutrition. Winston Churchill was spot on when he said that we make a living by what we get, but we make a life by what we give. How are you making a life? In what ways do you give your time, money and attention to those in need? Perhaps you offer your time at a local hospice or school, give money to some charitable causes, or help run a youth sports club. Whenever you give unconditionally and unreservedly without any expectation of anything in return, you are rewarded with a wonderful feeling of fulfilment.

You don't have to be rich to give. Bill and Melinda Gates may be able to give away billions of dollars, but you can always give your time. An hour a week helping at a local animal shelter or visiting an aged neighbour who lives alone is priceless.

Giving your time can be cathartic and humbling. Volunteering can shed you of all those status symbols you might be carrying around – job title, corner office, company car, influence and power. You're simply one volunteer among many serving soup or making beds. If you are suffering from thinking too highly of yourself, voluntary work can be a great way to bring you back down to earth.

Real success is about helping other people succeed.

16

Put it into action

Get started now

Start small if you must, but do something today. Avoid procrastinating – saying that you will start next week, next month or even next year. Money is always tight, so start with your time. No time to spare? I doubt it. What about getting up early at the weekends to volunteer a couple of hours? Nudge yourself to get started and within no time at all you will be surprised by how easily you have developed a new and altruistic habit.

Find causes that you believe in

You are not obliged to give your time, energy and resources. It is your choice. If you do choose to give, give to an organization, charity or cause that you feel passionate about helping. Explore and try to understand what your favourite charities or organizations represent. Ask your local charity shop how they spend the money collected before you volunteer to be a shop assistant. Watch a charity in action before committing to give it your time.

Start a trend

Lead the way in giving. Encourage those close to you to join with you. Share ideas with your family, friends and colleagues about how you might all volunteer for a particular cause. It is more fun to do things with others than alone. Your children might need a bit of persuasion to give up their beds, tablets or TVs but if they chose where you all volunteer your time they may be keener.

FOCUS ON THINGS YOU CAN CONTROL

'It makes no sense to worry about things you have no control over because there's nothing you can do about them, and why worry about things you do control? The activity of worrying keeps you immobilized.'

Wayne Dyer

Stop worrying about what you cannot control. It's a total waste of your energy, energy that could otherwise be used to help you focus on what you *can* influence. I spend large parts of my coaching sessions helping people to sift through their challenges and concerns – helping them to determine what they can change and what they have no control over. It always astonishes me how much time people spend trying to change what cannot be changed and then waste more energy complaining. The alternative is much more productive – simply focus on what is under your own control and influence.

What have you recently complained about that is beyond your control? It might be a period of bad weather, what your colleagues think about you or the fact that the holiday of your dreams is too expensive. When you're job hunting, do you moan about all the companies who never reply to your emails or do you explore how you can improve the process to increase the chances of success? If you're using a dating website, but your profile never gets seen, do you demand your money back or do you have a friend help you make your profile more appealing?

This process of deciding what is and what is not controllable is hard. Harder still when you have strong feelings about what is happening. But do you really want to waste your precious time focusing on the wrong things?

Stop worrying about what you cannot control.

17

Put it into action

Know the difference

'Grant me the strength to accept the things I cannot change, the courage to change the things I can, and the wisdom to know the difference.' Saint Francis of Assisi's famous words might have been written years ago but remain true today. Follow his advice and you are on the path to a more peaceful and fulfilling life.

Understand what is happening, be realistic about what is beyond your control and look to focus your attention on what you can do. You have the skills and tools you need: your free will, thoughts, reactions, emotions, mindset, ambitions and beliefs. If you use them wisely, you can respond to any challenge optimally – making the right decisions and interacting appropriately with others.

Start using your common sense to recognize when something cannot easily change, at least in the short term – for example, due to:

- other people's choices, decisions and emotional reactions
- the effects of group decisions such as stock market crashes and government policy
- the unexpected impact of so-called 'acts of God' such as bad weather
- unexpected events such as illnesses and accidents.

No more blame games

Avoid being in denial about what you can or cannot do. Do not keep blaming others:

- 'It is not my fault I overacted – he made me angry!'
- 'She forgot my birthday so why should I care about hers?'
- 'Nobody arrives on time so why should I make an effort to be early?'
- 'The team is not trying to achieve its goals so why should I try?'

It can take effort and practice but ultimately you are in control of your actions and choices.

LIVE WITHIN YOUR MEANS

'Your economic security does not lie in your job; it lies in your own power to produce – to think, to learn, to create, to adapt. That's true financial independence. It's not having wealth; it's having the power to produce wealth.'

Stephen Covey

Thirty-one per cent of British adults do not save anything and a further 32 per cent have less than £1,000 in savings. In addition, the average UK household has nearly £9,000 in unsecured debts (any debt excluding house or car loans). These statistics, garnered from surveys by Scottish Widows in 2012 and PwC in 2015, make for depressing reading.

You do not need to be a millionaire to feel successful or be successful. Financial wealth is only one of many possible indicators of success. However, to achieve your dreams and life goals you're going to need money. And making it requires financial planning and goal-setting. I do not know of any successful person who has been able to simply ignore their finances.

Your needs and desires change over time. You might not really know how much money you want to earn or save. Your answer today might simply be 'as much as possible', which is an OK answer if you earn more than you spend. The sad reality is that most people do the opposite. What borrowings or debts do you have? Are they above or below the £9,000 level mentioned earlier?

Having some debts can be a good thing: for example, taking out a mortgage loan to buy a house or apartment is investing in an asset that will hopefully increase in value over time and can also generate rental income.

Red lights should start flashing when you borrow money that you cannot easily pay off. Even more troubling is when you borrow simply to buy things for the house or to go on holiday – using your future income to consume more now.

...to achieve your dreams and life goals you're going to need money.

18

Put it into action

Set financial goals

It can be really grounding to understand where you are financially. Review with your partner or spouse the current state of your finances:

- What are your sources and amounts of income?
- How much do you spend on a regular basis and how much on one-off expenses?
- How much are you saving each month?
- What assets and debts do you have?

With this information as a starting point, write down your financial goals and dreams. You might want to buy a new house, retire in ten years or set money aside to pay for your children's school fees. How will you achieve these goals, to get you from where you are today to where you want to be? Do you need to find a higher-paying job or cut down on some expenses?

As you think of your future finances, do not simply follow other people's expectations. You do not have to emulate someone else's definition of financial success. Have your own financial goals.

Defer consumption

Do not be embarrassed or shy about not spending. You don't have to keep up with your friends and neighbours as they buy new clothes, cars or home furnishings. In the words of US president Calvin Coolidge, 'There is no dignity quite so impressive, and no one independence quite so important, as living within your means.' Saving and/or investing some of your current income is an essential part of anyone's financial goals. Automatically transfer the amount you want to save or invest into a fixed-deposit account as soon as you receive your monthly salary. You must then live on the remainder and spend less than you used to. Avoid the temptation to buy now and pay later – through credit cards or hire-purchase offers. Only spend today what you have today.

LIVE IN THE 'REAL WORLD'

'Turn off your email; turn off your phone; disconnect from the Internet; figure out a way
to set limits so you can concentrate when you need to, and disengage when you need to.
Technology is a good servant but a bad master.'

Gretchen Rubin

Too much time online can cause mental illness. This was the conclusion of a study reported
in the *Mirror* newspaper in May 2014. Various articles and surveys link time spent 'online'
with all kinds of problems – depression, suicide, loneliness, poor social skills, low self-
esteem, lack of physical exercise and losing touch with reality.

But how do you come 'offline' when so much of our daily lives is moving 'online'? Every
month new sites and online services are launched. If you need to check anything – about
a new school for your children, medical treatment, tourist destination or recipe – you go
online. Bill Gates put it so well when he called the Internet the 'town square for the global
village of tomorrow'.

Could you spend a week or even a day without reading your emails, using social media or
going online? Someone recently joked with me that having Internet access is more important than having food or water! In one Mashable survey, 24 per cent of recipients admitted
to missing important moments in person because they were too busy trying to share those
same moments on social media. Does this sound familiar? You take photos of something
so as to post it immediately on Instagram rather than experiencing what's happening in
front of your eyes.

I recently saw two people bump into each other on the street. Both had been looking at
their smartphones rather than where they were going. At a recent party I looked around
and observed that more people were looking at their screens than talking with those next
to them. I felt embarrassed having to interrupt one of the partygoers as they typed away on
their phone. I only wanted a normal face-to-face conversation!

Take the time to experience what's happening in front of your eyes.

19

Put it into action

Curb your time online

The Internet is a wonderful thing but you have to keep a balance between being online and offline. How many hours a day do you spend online catching up on Facebook, viewing photos on Instagram, talking on WhatsApp or surfing websites?

- Try switching off your phone's mobile Internet access, only accessing the web via wireless in your home, office or coffee shop. You can now walk down the street enjoying the view and not feeling compelled to be looking down at your phone's screen every time you hear a beep.
- Invite friends to your home and insist that everyone leaves their phones in their pockets and handbags.
- Each day call someone on the phone rather than speaking with them via Facebook Messenger or WhatsApp. Have a proper conversation rather than simply talking in short abbreviated sentences interspersed with emojis.
- Write someone a letter or a card. Your handwriting is very personal and conveys emotions and warmth.
- Have a break from searching on Google. Spend a couple of hours at a bookstore or library just browsing. Rediscover the joys that come from leafing through books and magazines.
- At weekends and on holiday have entire days with no Internet access. Take photos but only post them on social media the following day. Simply enjoy your surroundings without the urge to tell the world.

STAY FOCUSED

'Bees cannot sting and make honey at the same time. They have to make a choice. Either
they are going to be a stinger or a honey-maker.'

Emanuel Cleaver

Success requires a focused attention of your time and energy. This is true no matter what you want to achieve – to change the world or simply change apartments. All success stories come down to one person having a focused aim – so focused at times it can look like an obsession.

J.K. Rowling spent her days writing, even while she had little money and poverty loomed. This single-minded focus gave the world Harry Potter and brought her untold wealth and success. The same could be said of Mo Farah or Steve Jobs. None of these people tried to achieve multiple goals and objectives on their early roads to success. None of them spread themselves too thin. Farah had a clear middle-distance running focus. Jobs focused on a single business start-up from his garage. He did not create Apple while simultaneously setting up half a dozen other business ventures. These are all examples of singleness of purpose, which, to quote John D. Rockefeller, is one of the chief essentials for success in life, no matter what your ultimate aim.

Unfortunately, life has a habit of throwing all kinds of activities and responsibilities at us, forcing us to spend our days multi-tasking. Even when this happens, you can still be focused – on each job as you tackle it. The only way to ensure success is by giving each activity your full undivided attention for as long as needed. It is a fallacy to believe that you can successfully multi-task in any other way.

All success stories come down to one person having a focused aim.

Put it into action

Set an example by doing one thing at a time

Stop trying to be a Jack-of-all-trades and be a master of one thing. Whether it's writing an email, kicking a ball around with your kids, driving through the city or simply being alone and meditating. For those ten minutes you're doing something – or for whatever period of time it takes – do it with 100-per-cent focus. The new disease of our age is being OK doing everything at exactly the same time.

Our children think they are very good at such multi-tasking – my son listens to music, while completing homework and having a WhatsApp conversation with friends. Set an example to people around you – when someone calls you, stop everything else and speak to them. If you can't at that moment, call them back later. Avoid the terrible habit of speaking on the phone and simultaneously writing on your computer, watching TV or driving on a busy road.

Turn down other people's requests

You do not need to be all things to all people. The easiest way to spread yourself too thin is by taking on board the needs and requests of other people. Learn to push back – ideally, gently and diplomatically. Of course, you will often want to help others – family, friends, colleagues, neighbours – but you need to learn balance. You need to know when to accept and when to decline. Will this be hard for you? Do you struggle to say 'no'? Try to be honest with people and explain how busy you are. People will understand if you tell them you simply do not have the bandwidth.

LOVE MORE

Love is either a wonderful thing or a psychological disorder depending on your perspective. One thing is clear: successful people are powered by love as a positive force.

When coaching people, I find it helpful to view love as two distinct groups of experiences: momentary love and sustainable love.

Momentary love can take many forms including infatuation, passion, need, lust or a desire for possession. You see it in impulse purchases, a passionate fling or longing for a new car or toy. Often based around wanting someone or something, such moments or feelings of love make you feel great but do not last. They *never* last. You might try to make them last by continually buying new shoes or having affairs. Chasing these moments is just a way to fill a void you have in yourself – perhaps reflecting low self-esteem, lack of self-confidence or some other issue that you carry around with you. Seeking this kind of love might give you 'successful' moments but is no basis for a genuinely successful life.

Sustainable love can appear unexciting and less cool than momentary love but do not be fooled by appearances. This is what you need to create a truly successful life. It is what you feel and experience in meaningful relationships – those relationships where you truly accept and connect with yourself and others – with family, partners, children, colleagues and friends. Developing these relationships can be hard. The temptation to walk away is often in the air but, if you persevere, you will be rewarded.

On which kind of love have you been focusing your time and energy?

...successful people are powered by love...

21

Put it into action

Love yourself

The secret to your success lies in surrounding yourself with sustainable love, and that starts with loving yourself. This is your hardest challenge. Through hundreds of hours spent coaching I have observed a common pattern – we can easily express our love for other people, possessions or experiences but find it difficult to say we love ourselves. You must have heard comments such as:

- 'I hate myself for staying in this relationship.'
- 'I am angry with myself for not finding a higher-paying job.'
- 'I loathe myself for always being mean to my parents.'
- 'I keep beating myself up for not being more ambitious.'

To love yourself involves understanding, acceptance, forgiveness and being at peace with who you are. To be comfortable and at peace with yourself you need to:

- understand that none of us is perfect and you are not the only one who has faults, weaknesses and issues
- accept yourself as you are, no matter how imperfect you think yourself to be
- forgive yourself and stop blaming yourself for errors and mistakes in your life.

Change your love focus

From today, start relying less upon momentary love with all its appealing pleasures and gratifications and instead invest more time in sustainable love. Are you able to do so? Be honest and look at your life – are you constantly seeking highs, new thrills and experiences?

As you step away from short-term momentary experiences of love, fill the space with as much sustainable love as you are able. Spend more time and effort in relationships that matter. It is easy to do as long as you are willing. Your capacity to create and to grow sustainable love in your life is unlimited.

REINVENT YOURSELF

'Invent yourself and then reinvent yourself ... and reinvent your life because you must; it is
your life and its history and the present belong only to you.'

Charles Bukowski

Have you ever felt that it's time to change? Time to press your reboot button? You're not
alone – we all do. Think back over what's got you to where you are and you'll see many
moments of reinvention. They may not have felt like a big deal at the time and sometimes
you only realize what has happened after the event.

Reinventions can take different forms:

- resigning from a job to move in a new career direction
- going back to school to learn something new
- moving away from certain friends and connecting with new people
- going from being a carefree single person to settling down
- choosing to change aspects of your personality or character
- giving away old clothes and buying a new-look wardrobe
- making a decision to leave somewhere you have lived for years
- allowing your relationship and interaction with family members to change.

Sometimes planning a major change or U-turn in life can leave you with feelings of guilt;
a sense that you have failed somehow or been forced to start over. Do not feel guilty or
embarrassed. Reinventing yourself is an essential process if you want to grow and flourish.
As we age and mature we learn and experience so much and it is inevitable that our goals,
plans and expectations change. Embrace change and try to ensure that it builds on your
successes to date. In the words of singer and writer Auliq Ice, 'Rather than trying to reinvent
the wheel, build on that which is already excellent in your life.'

Reinventing yourself is an essential process if you want to grow and flourish.

22

Put it into action

Be proactive in your self-reinvention

Sometimes changes are forced upon us. Stress and burnout lead us to change jobs or career direction. Anger, arguments and bitterness lead to divorce. Health problems lead to changes of lifestyle. You don't need to wait for drastic events to start a major change in your life. Sit down on a regular basis and explore where you are now. Brainstorm these questions:

To have a more successful life...

- What should I stop doing, thinking and being?
- What should I start doing, thinking and being?
- What could I do, think and be less of?
- What could I do, think and be more of?
- And, finally, what could I do, think and be differently?

Draw and write your answers as doodles or a mind map. From this you will see where you might need to reinvent yourself.

Reinvention can be costly and lonely

Do seek the thoughts and opinions of people whose advice you really value and trust but be prepared for the fact that they may not agree with you. You may even lose friends if they don't understand your desire to change part of your life.

You also need to be ready to walk away from aspects of your life that you have invested time and effort in, such as a particular career path or relationship.

STAY HEALTHY

'If you have health, you probably will be happy, and if you have health and happiness, you
have all the wealth you need, even if it is not all you want.'

Elbert Hubbard

Where is the sense in working too hard, getting over-stressed and burning out, just to
earn enough money to pay for your healthcare? I see this play out all too often in the
lives of people I have worked with. I have heard some very odd things during my coaching
conversations:

- 'I have no time to exercise or to eat a healthy lunch, but that is common in my line of work.'
- 'I will just keep going at 110 per cent for a few more years, then I will retire and relax.'
- 'If I slow down and live a more healthy life, how can I support my family? They have
  certain financial needs and expectations.'
- 'I know that I am overweight but at my age it seems too late to start exercising now.'

So many of us, it seems, are planning to focus on our health when we've finished working and making money. Well, don't hold your breath. Sadly, evidence suggests that your
health is probably going to decline very quickly once you retire. A 2013 IEA study in the UK
concluded that 'being retired decreases physical, mental and self-assessed health'. Don't be
banking too much on using all of that free time you're suddenly going to have to become
healthier.

Working yourself into the ground serves no one. It only decreases your chances of living
a long and healthy life. Do you really want to sacrifice your health and long life for a big
house, fancy car and hefty bank account?

> Where is the sense in working too hard just to pay for your healthcare?

23

Put it into action

Treat your health as your main wealth

The thing about money is that you can have bad years and even lose it all and then make it all back again the following year. If you go bankrupt with your health, you won't be earning it back any time soon. Your health needs to be positively maintained all the time. You need to commit to looking after the different aspects of your health throughout your life.

- Exercise, stretch, walk, swim or run. If you need support and encouragement, seek it. Hire a personal trainer, join a running club, or find a friend to swim with. Do whatever it takes to maintain your physical health. Get into the habit of walking each day. A recent UK study showed that a daily 20-minute brisk walk adds seven years to your life and substantially reduces your risk of a heart attack.
- Maintain your mental health by avoiding excessive stress, overwork, worry, anxiety and burnout. Often, the answer lies in finding a balance and not overdoing things. Do so before your body starts to feel your mental anguish through back aches and stiff necks.
- Walk away from people and situations that emotionally drain you. Value your emotional health. Perhaps it is a jealous colleague, a micro-managing boss or a family member who is always bringing you down. Being emotionally weakened can affect your physical health.
- Try to maintain your spiritual health by finding meaning in things you do. Avoid activities that you find meaningless or fill you with boredom, apathy and a sense that you are wasting your time. As with mental and emotional ill health, this can weaken your body.

FORGIVE OTHERS

'To forgive is to set a prisoner free and discover that the prisoner was you.'

Louis B. Smedes

Refusing to forgive never made anyone feel better about anything. All you are doing is holding on to feelings of upset, anger and jealousy and that can never be good. I once read that being angry and unforgiving towards someone else is like drinking poison and expecting the other person to die.

To create a successful life you must forgive others who have hurt or offended you. Not because they were right or because you can forget what they have done, but because forgiving frees you up to live a more full and positive life. By forgiving, you allow yourself to move on. You release yourself from a self-imposed prison of negative feelings. This is very important to understand – you must forgive others for the sake of your own wellbeing.

Forgiving others isn't weak, proof that you were not really hurt or that you were wrong to have been angry. What you are really doing when you forgive others is saying, 'I no longer need to waste my emotions and feelings on you and how you acted.' You are showing the strength to move on. When coaching people, I often find that my role is to help them let go and move on by forgiving others and also themselves.

Forgiving often goes hand in hand with learning to trust again. When something bad happens in a relationship you can choose to walk away or try to rebuild it. Forgiveness removes the negative feelings of mistrust and allows relationships to be rebuilt.

To create a successful life you must forgive others who have hurt or offended you.

24

Put it into action

Be honest where forgiveness is needed

Too often we fool ourselves into thinking we have nothing to forgive others for:

- 'Of course, I am not angry that I missed out on a promotion at work.'
- 'It is fine that my colleague stole my idea and presented it as her own.'
- 'No, I am not hurt at all by my partner's infidelity.'

Think about what has hurt you that you may be denying. Be honest with yourself. By all means pretend to others that you are fine – at times, we do not want to reveal our true feelings, and that's fine.

Your challenge is to find the moment and timing to forgive the other person. It might take you days, weeks or even longer. You might find it helpful to talk about your feelings and the question of forgiveness with someone you trust.

Find your own way to forgive

How you forgive is your personal choice but you must always start by agreeing with yourself that you are ready to forgive. In some instances, you might decide to tell the other party. It can be therapeutic to actually write to that person. It does not matter whether they want or need such forgiveness. Alternatively, you may tell only your family and friends that you have moved on and forgive a particular person. All that is important is that you let go and release all those negative feelings that become bottled up from not having forgiven someone.

BE PART OF A TRIBE

'For millions of years, human beings have been part of one tribe or another. A group needs
only two things to be a tribe: a shared interest and a way to communicate.'

Seth Godin

Without even realizing it, you spend your life as part of many different tribes. Tribes are
all those informal and formal groups of people that have things in common – things that
bind you all together. You are born into tribes, then join them by virtue of where you live,
your career and your various activities. Everywhere you look you can see examples – family,
social circles, work colleagues, religious groups, charity volunteers, sports clubs, regulars in
a pub, college classmates, people living in the same building or village.

Think for a moment about your own life and with whom you associate and interact. What
do members of each of your different social groups have in common? Is it...

- family interests and loyalty?
- love of football?
- working in the same department?
- enjoying the same village pub?
- friends from university days?
- sharing the same local gym?
- community living in an apartment building?
- living together in the same old people's home?

Perhaps you are someone who avoids being in any tribes at all, or who is a member of only
those tribes that you are compelled to be part of – your group of work colleagues, your college
class or your family. Only the hermit in a distant cave can claim to be free of any tribes at all.

Being part of tribal groupings enables you to interact with others and to make friends. It
can give life meaning through a sense of belonging. You belong somewhere. We all do.
A sense of belonging is important. You will probably balance this with time alone to reflect,
recharge and be with yourself. If you are more shy or introverted, you may like being in your
own space more than in others'.

A sense of belonging is important.

25

Put it into action

Choose your groups wisely

Take a few minutes to list all of those 'tribes' that you are part of. Look through what you have written, asking yourself:

- 'How do I benefit and contribute to this or that tribe? Is it good for me to be involved?'
- 'In what ways might being part of this tribe be bad for me? Is it holding me back in some way?'
- 'Is it time for me to move on from a tribe? Am I able to?'
- 'Which other tribes should I become part of? Will I be able to join?'

You might be surprised by what you conclude:

- It might be time for you to step back from your micro-managing parents or jealous siblings, by spending less time with your 'family tribe'.
- You might realize that you are neglecting to get to know your neighbours, in what could be called your 'community tribe'.
- It might be time to take up the many offers from your work colleagues to join them on their social outings.
- You might be job hunting and decide to join the local chapter of your university's alumni association.

Your time on this planet is limited. Spend it with people you love, like or have an interest in connecting with. Stop wasting your time and energy with people who mean nothing to you or who bring you down. Let yourself be drawn to people who uplift you, make you feel good and whom you are happy to be around.

EXUDE CONFIDENCE

'If you believe in yourself and feel confident in yourself, you can do anything.
I really believe that.'

Karlie Kloss

If you are comfortable and happy with who you are, then you have the kind of confidence you need for a successful life. It is about being truly OK with who you are, what you are doing and where you are heading. It is about knowing what you know, what you do not know and being willing to say so. It is typified by a quote I recently read: 'I used to walk into a room full of people and wonder if they liked me; now I look around and wonder if I like them.'

This type of confidence isn't noisy or necessarily extrovert and it's not about social skills or smooth talking. It's about being completely at peace with yourself.

In reality, your confidence probably rises and falls depending on what's happening around you. Most of us would feel a wobble at comments like:

- 'What, you haven't completed writing your report yet? I have and have sent it to our boss who loves all of my new ideas.'
- 'Wow, you weren't selected for the sports team? I guess you didn't train enough though. Better luck next season.'

Try not to let your confidence be weakened by minor knocks, and recognize when other people are trying to put you down and make you feel small. Comments like these can make you upset, angry, jealous, even tearful. This is normal. But you must not let them eat into your inner confidence, the confidence based on how you value yourself – believe in yourself regardless of what other people say about you.

> True confidence is about being completely at peace with yourself.

26

Put it into action

Facing new situations

Really confident people know that there will be times when they don't feel that confident. Facing new situations and challenges can be difficult. Give yourself permission to feel unsure and unclear. No one is perfect. Nobody has all the answers. In situations like this it is OK to say 'I am not confident.' Give yourself the necessary settling in time to be able to know what you need to do or where you need to go. Allow your confidence in a new situation to emerge.

Acting confident builds your confidence

When coaching people I often say that, if you want to do something differently, you may need to 'fake it until you make it'. What this means is acting as if you have already acquired the skills you need. This can be applied to confidence very effectively. Try the following. Act as if...

• you are comfortable and happy with who you are
• you are OK with what you are doing
• you are OK with where you are heading.

People around you will have no idea you are putting on an act. By appearing confident, other people will be more comfortable connecting, working and being with you. Confidence is contagious, too. As you act more confident with yourself, you give other people the permission and courage to do the same.

Do not feel guilty putting up a front. Even the most super-confident people in the world are acting a little to maintain the air of absolute confidence.

GIVE CREDIT WHERE IT'S DUE

> 'Giving credit where credit is due is a very rewarding habit to form. Its rewards are inestimable.'
>
> Loretta Young

One of the main reasons for divorces and job resignations isn't falling out or cheating. Surveys have shown that break-ups happen because people don't get the credit they feel they are due. Everyone wants to be acknowledged. It stems from our human need to be valued, recognized and loved. Thanking people regularly and acknowledging their efforts are hugely important.

Giving credit can take two forms – private and public – but whether you say thanks through a one-to-one meeting, a personal email or a shout from the rooftops – make sure that you do it. There is a huge power in a few simple words of thanks.

Some people have a greater need for thanks than others, something that is linked to personality and upbringing. Are you someone who needs to be given credit? How do you feel when you don't get it for something you've done?

Actually, there is something worse than not being given credit and that is when someone else is takes the credit for something you've done. If this happens to you, try challenging the person who has done it. See whether they apologize or deny it.

There is a huge power in a few simple words of thanks.

27

Put it into action

Make it a daily habit

Be open and ready to recognize people in and outside work. Try to make it a daily habit to compliment, thank and credit people around you. You don't need to wait for something large and obvious to acknowledge. Allow small and inconsequential things to get your attention.

Show appreciation in words and actions. Try one of these and see what happens:

- Take a colleague to one side and thank them for something they've done in the last week.
- Send your partner flowers or chocolates to thank them for a lovely weekend.
- Buy your assistant a coffee to show that you appreciate them working late on something urgent.
- Send an email round your department to recognize a junior member of the team who has just come up with a new idea.

Recognition is infectious. It is a sure-fire way to make those around you feel more positive, and more positive towards you. You will get a reputation for being caring, observant, grateful and appreciative – qualities that most people do not experience enough in their lives.

Even if *you* do not need recognition, understand that others do

Most people love being complimented, thanked and recognized. They feel motivated and energized by the attention. If you are one of them, you'll instantly understand the benefits of giving credit.

If it's not something you need, you'll have to make an extra effort to make sure that you do not overlook giving credit to those around you. If you forget, simply apologize and try to make amends immediately. Late is always better than never.

REDUCE ATTACHMENTS TO POSSESSIONS

'I am convinced that material things can contribute a lot to making one's life pleasant, but, basically, if you do not have very good friends and relatives who matter to you, life will be really empty and sad and material things cease to be important.'

David Rockefeller

You are not your material possessions. They do not define who you really are. Your nice car, house, clothes, flat-screen TV, designer shoes and bank account are not your source of happiness. All evidence – anecdotal and from surveys – confirms this. Sure, you may be thrilled and excited by a sleek new car or racing bike but after the initial euphoria wears off, what then? Are you happier than you were before because of your new possession? Are you really more successful as a result?

If you are very poor, then material possessions can give you a higher level of comfort, happiness and self-fulfilment – in fact, they can radically change your life – but as you acquire more and upgrade your possessions, they will have no impact on your level of happiness.

Be honest with yourself about why you want to buy a new car or move to a larger house. Be careful about trying to demonstrate success through possessions. It is OK to aspire to own and buy whatever you want but be honest with yourself about your motivations. Successful people don't need possessions to prove their success.

You are not your material possessions.

28

Put it into action

Take an audit of what you own

Do an audit of the stuff you have in your wardrobe, cupboards, garage or spare room. Count how many shirts, books or pairs of shoes you have. If your home or office is so cluttered that you do not know where to start, then you need to take drastic action. Think about how useful all your stuff is. Do you have anything you've bought, used it once, then forgotten all about it? Do you have anything still in its original packaging?

Simplify your life and give it away

Ask yourself what you really need. There is a lot of talk these days about simplifying your life and leading a more minimalist way of life and this is your chance to get started. What is essential and what can you live without? Give away your extra shoes, toys, clothes or furniture.

Why not adopt a system where, if you buy something new, you have to give away or sell something else. Recycle your old clothes so that they can go to refugees or the homeless. Give books to a local coffee shop or charity.

Don't look back

Ask yourself why you have acquired so much stuff. What are the patterns in how and why you buy things? Are you a hoarder, or do you just love shopping? Think about which of your buying habits need changing. You could save yourself a lot of money and space.

BUILD RAPPORT

'The most basic and powerful way to connect to another person is to listen. Just listen.
Perhaps the most important thing we ever give each other is our attention.'

Rachel Naomi Remen

It is impossible to be successful without building rapport. Rapport is the essential process of understanding one other and becoming comfortable together. Success comes from having people follow you, work with you, support you and believe in you. For this to happen, people need to understand, trust and be aligned with you. They need to be comfortable being with you. This happens automatically if you have built rapport. It can happen without you even realizing it through your daily interactions, but sometimes it takes a bit more work.

I sense that women are more natural at building rapport than men. When women communicate with others they normally speak more slowly, listen more and show empathy – all classic rapport-building skills. I read a lovely quote by Deborah Tannen on this point: 'For most women, the language of conversation is primarily a language of rapport: a way of establishing connections and negotiating relationships.' Men, take note – you might have to try a bit harder.

You may not be able to create rapport with everybody – you may not even want to. There will always be people you find too selfish or self-absorbed or just too boring and not worth knowing. If it's someone you regularly cross paths with, however, do try to build some rapport. You don't want the person to feel that you are being rude or cold and trying to ignore them.

It is impossible to be successful without building rapport.

29

Put it into action

Find common ground

A foundation for lasting rapport is that you find common ground with others. Spend time understanding what they are thinking, expecting, doing and believing. You can then see where you have similarities and where you are in alignment. It could be something as simple as your opinions about a friend or colleague, your hobbies or your career goals. Try to be authentic – never agree with someone or claim to like what they like just to please them.

Align yourself

Make the other person comfortable in your presence by acting the same way as them. Mirroring is an incredibly powerful technique for building rapport. If they are standing, stand with them. If they are sitting with arms and legs crossed, do the same. This is called 'postural congruence'. It is a great way of helping someone else to feel comfortable with you at an unconscious level. In most cases, they won't even realize you're copying them. Try this out as soon as you can.

Listen well and show empathy

Be someone other people want to be around. Avoid being selfish and talking about yourself and instead learn about the other person. Remain calm and speak slowly. By doing all of these things you will appear warm and people will want to know you.

LIVE MINDFULLY

'Mindfulness is simply being aware of what is happening right now without wishing it were different.'

James Baraz

There are plans under way for dangerous prisoners in Britain to be taught mindfulness-based techniques to help calm their violent impulses. In the corporate world, courses and training in living and working mindfully are increasingly being provided to employees.

Mindfulness is simply about being in the moment and, by being completely in the moment, cutting off worries about your past or stress about the future. It is about calmly paying attention to what is happening to you now. To repeat the old cliché, it is about waking up and smelling the roses.

At its core is a call for you to be calm and at peace with what is happening rather than worrying about what could happen, what went wrong, or what is missing. We are all experts at letting our thoughts and concerns take us away from what's happening in the present moment. If you've ever distractedly driven your car and got to your destination without any recollection of the drive, you'll know what this feels like.

Being mindful is about you letting the past stay in the past and leaving the future as something yet to happen. it's about just being in the present moment without any worries about what might happen or what has already happened to cloud it.

Being mindful is a process of letting go and shedding habits of:

- thinking about the past and feeling guilty about things you did not do
- worrying about what might happen tomorrow or next week
- being afraid to do something today for fear of how it will play out tomorrow.

Being mindful is about you letting the past stay in the past and leaving the future as something yet to happen.

30

Put it into action

Become a friend of your thoughts

You may never be able to silence the thousands of thoughts that pass through your mind each day uninvited and unexpected, but you can get some peace and reduce the distraction. Your goal is to:

- stop giving attention to all of your thoughts
- slow down the number of thoughts that pass through your mind.

Take up meditation and learn to silence and slow down your mind. There are many methods or styles to choose from, so find a type that works for you. It could be with music or a guided meditation either in person, on a CD or using YouTube.

During meditation learn to let your thoughts come and go; allow them to pass through your mind without building internal conversations around them. Allow moments of silence to exist between each thought. Learn to enjoy being in quiet moments where you can simply focus on your breathing and on your body. Through regular meditation you will find yourself slowly becoming calmer and more able to live in the present; less concerned and focused on what has happened or could happen.

Slow down to appreciate small moments

Pause and look around you. Learn to observe what is happening. Train your mind to give your attention to what is happening now, what you are feeling now. Don't give your mind the time and space to return to its worries about yesterday and tomorrow. Find as many moments as possible to give your mind a rest from its continual and incessant worrying. When eating a meal in a restaurant or at home, simply enjoy the food, company and surroundings. Do not worry about how much it will cost, how hard it was for you to cook or the time you will spend washing the dishes.

ACCEPT COMPROMISES

'Any relationship (friend, romantic or business) that's one sided isn't one; it's a one-way street headed in one direction ... nowhere.'

T. F. Hodge

We love to talk about win–win decisions. In truth, they are often lose–lose compromises – not having everything that you want in return for allowing someone else not to have everything they want. We spend our lives making compromises, and they are often the best way forward. Some are easy – where to eat dinner, which film to watch at the cinema, which venue to host a team off-site or who speaks first at a sales presentation. More meaningful decisions around the big things in life – changing jobs, getting married, buying a house, having children – are more challenging. With these, reaching compromise can be hard.

These types of choices go to the heart of who we are – our ambitions, dreams and life goals – the things that symbolize our identity. It is not easy to compromise and be flexible with these. But compromise is essential for the sake of the people close to you and the important relationships in your life. It is highly unlikely that your life goals and ambitions are identical to those of the people who count in your life. As a result, there will be moments when your needs and goals will conflict. I recently coached a leader who had been offered a promotion but only if he would quickly relocate to Singapore. He wanted to accept the offer but his wife loved her work in London and their children had just settled into new schools there. Scenarios like these call for mature discussion and compromise.

How often have you faced such critical decisions that involve those closest to you?

...compromise is essential for the sake of the people close to you and the important relationships in your life.

31

Put it into action

Let things go

Remember the merits of compromise. Giving in can often be a good decision for you and your relationships. Unfortunately, when emotions and tensions run high it creates pressure and gives you little time to think. Remember:

- You do not have to be right. Be honest with yourself about what is motivating you – and don't just stubbornly hold out from a pure desire to win.
- Think about how important the outcome is for you and how flexible you can be in searching for compromises.
- Be willing to learn and change. Be creative in looking for solutions that can work for all parties. Be ready to try something new. This might start with you openly sharing your feelings and concerns.

Know when compromise is not an option

The secret is knowing when to give and take and when to hold firm. Think through the situation and act based on understanding the likely effects of your decision. Consider this question: how important is your need to win compared to value of the relationship? If in doubt, find a compromise.

If compromise is not possible, when your values, ethics and integrity are being challenged, you should stand firm. It is not a good idea to compromise on your primary beliefs.

BE MORE THAN YOUR 9-5

'Do you work to live or live to work? If you love your work, it doesn't really matter.'
Mary-Frances Winters

'What do you do for a living?' How many times have you heard that when you meet new people? It's a question that compels you to talk about your job and work, putting you in a box and ignoring everything else that makes you you. For a while I answered the question by saying 'I spend my time smiling' but that only delayed the inevitable.

If you are with people who are talking about their careers and high-profile jobs, it can be uncomfortable to explain that you are stay-at-home parent, a mature student or in-between jobs right now. You might feel you have little to contribute.

But does telling someone about your job really capture and explain who you are? If you live to work, then probably yes, it does. You would be happy to be defined as 'that person in that role in that organization'. But most people aren't like this; they are the total opposite. Most people work to live. They aren't passionate about what they do – they might actually find it boring or beneath them.

The important thing to remember is that work is only one aspect of who you are; one part of how you choose to live your life. Even if you claim that your job is everything and you are very successful at it, is it really success if you're doing it to the exclusion of everything else?

...work is only one aspect of who you are...

32

Put it into action

Define who you want to be

Decide what *you* want to be known for. Forget other people's priorities for a moment and think about yours. If the grand-sounding job titles that matter to other people don't matter to you, what is important?

Write down your priorities. Be honest about them. Your list should reflect what *you* care about, not what other people care about. When you've finished, turn this list into the story you'll tell next time someone asks you what you do. It's human nature to love stories and whatever you say will be far more interesting than a job title or impressive-sounding employer.

Success is success

Throw away the common perception that work and career success are somehow greater in stature, prestige and importance than successes in other parts of your life. Success is also about bringing up a family, doing charity work, renovating your home, studying part-time for a university degree, coaching your children's sports teams or painting portraits. Your successes are your successes. Be proud of whatever they are – it does not matter if and how other people recognize them. The world would be such a dull and boring place if people focused all their energy only on their careers and their 9–5 jobs.

Choose what works for you

The secret is to achieve a conscious balance – a balance between the importance of your work and the importance of other aspects of your life. Make conscious choices about how you spend your time and effort:

- Could working part-time be a way for you to write that first novel?
- Could holding down two jobs for a short time help you earn the money to retrain for your dream career?

KNOW YOURSELF

'Man's main task in life is to give birth to himself, to become what he potentially is. The most important product of his effort is his own personality.'

Erich Fromm

When you're driving a car you have to be careful of blind spots – those areas you miss when looking in the side mirrors. The same applies with your personality. It is very hard to live a successful life being blind to parts of your own personality, no matter how uncomfortable those parts may make you feel. When I coach people I always say, 'Isn't it better to know what other people already know about you? Why stay blind to how you are perceived?'

Learn more about your personality by asking people for their opinions and feedback. You could take a personality test or use a psychometric assessment tool such as the MBTI, DISC or Harrison Assessment. Typically based on you completing a questionnaire, the results can be very revealing.

Once you understand yourself better, you will be able to optimize your personality through maximizing your strengths and managing your weaknesses. We each have some natural or developed strengths in how we interact, work and communicate. Make best use of them and ensure that they do not become weaknesses. Confidence, for example, can be an enormous advantage but you have to ensure that it does not tip over into arrogance.

Weaker areas of our personality can be hard to totally eliminate. We can all be impatient, over-sensitive and emotional at times, and these are not easy personality traits to change. The secret is to be careful in situations where a weakness might undermine you. Learn to recognize when you need to make an extra effort to be patient or thick-skinned.

Get to know what other people already know about you.

33

Put it into action

Assess your own personality

When was the last time you looked at your own personality? Spend a moment now to review your unique combination of behaviours, traits, psyche, style and mindset. Every day people around you observe and experience these things when interacting with you. Now it's time for you to reflect on what they really see.

How would your family, friend and colleagues describe you if I were to ask them to describe you? Are you:

- outgoing and extrovert or quiet and reflective?
- impulsive or measured?
- emotional or rational?
- a good listener or someone who loves hearing their own voice?
- positive and happy or easily depressed by negative events happening around you?

It's more than likely that you exhibit different personalities in different situations. Many of us have a personality at home and another at work. Try to understand how people in different contexts see you.

While you are reviewing your personality traits, be aware that whenever you do something that involves other people or emotions you will reveal different elements of your personality – for example, when:

- put under stress by your boss
- driving in a traffic jam
- asked to lead a difficult meeting
- giving someone bad news
- speaking in public to a large group.

Other people can be very good at describing us. Those closest to us can be frightening in how well they know us. The million-dollar question is how well do you know yourself?

EMBRACE THE JOURNEY OF GETTING OLDER

'Since our society equates happiness with youth, we often assume that sorrow, quiet desperation, and hopelessness go hand in hand with getting older. They don't. Emotional pain or numbness are symptoms of living the wrong life, not a long life.'

Martha Beck

Stop crying over what you have lost and start enjoying what you have gained. We live in a world where youth is idolized and success seems to come to young people only in their teens, twenties and maybe thirties. They seem to be the ones who break records, earn millions, write bestsellers and lead high-growth start-up companies.

Every one of us spends too long looking back. People in their twenties long for the life of a carefree student. People in their forties miss the uncomplicated, responsibility-free days of their thirties. People in their sixties regret missing the chance to achieve new career and life dreams.

It's time to stop all this longingly looking backwards to those good old days. Getting old is a good thing. Embrace your ageing and open your eyes to the amazing opportunities it affords you. I am close to reaching my half-century and I truly understand the range of feelings that you face as each year passes. Instead of concentrating on what you're losing as you age, focus on what you're gaining – experience, insight, wisdom, new opportunities and adventures you never had time for before.

Don't live in denial about your age or try to fight it with short-term distractions that give you the illusion of escape. Embrace it.

Stop crying over what you have lost and start enjoying what you have gained.

34

Put it into action

Let go of who you were

Act young by all means. In fact, please act young – be youthful and relive activities from your younger days – but remember you can never again be that version of yourself. You have lived beyond that period of your life. You have experienced much since then, observed what comes later and have the benefit of hindsight.

Embrace what you have become

The secret is to embrace what you have become while allowing yourself to remain connected with who you were. Be comfortable being all ages. Be what you have become while allowing yourself to revisit your youth.

Think now about the incredible range of life experiences you have gained from having 'been there and done that'. Be content that you have already been through so many events and moments, which those younger than you have yet to face.

Think about the wisdom you have gained from having been through the ups and down of life with all its joys and pains. Do not underestimate the amazing understanding of people and the world around you that this wisdom affords.

It's never too late to change

The saddest thing is for someone to feel too old to aspire to something. I have lost count of how many times I have coached someone who has allowed their age to be their excuse. It isn't really your age that holds you back; it is your mind, full of fears and concerns of failure, scared of being shown up, and scared sometimes of actually succeeding.

BE BOTH AN EXTROVERT AND AN INTROVERT

'An extrovert looks at a stack of books and sees a stack of papers, while an introvert looks at the same stack and sees a soothing source of escape.'

Eric Samuel Timm

Are you an extrovert or an introvert? The common perception is that extroverts are confident, loud and fond of public speaking, while introverts are the shy, quiet people in the background. This is wrong. A true extrovert is someone who likes to talk through what they are thinking, likes to spend time with others and to learn through doing things. A true introvert likes to think before speaking, listens well, is happy in their own space and reflects on ideas before acting. An extrovert can appear just as shy or as confident as an introvert.

According to well-researched psychology going back to the work of Carl Jung, we are born one or the other. You might already know your personality type through the famous Myers–Briggs Type Indicator (MBTI). We all exhibit a combination of both styles but each of us is predominantly one or the other. This dominant style is what other people see us as.

The key to your success is to consciously adopt the style that's right for the situation you are in – to draw upon either extroversion or introversion when needed from your toolkit. The goal isn't to lose your natural style – that's very much who you are. Instead, it's just to sometimes step out of your automatic and natural way of being. Sometimes the quiet person needs to speak up more to be heard, while the person who dominates meetings decides to take a back seat and allow others to express their ideas.

> The key to your success is to consciously adopt the style that's right for the situation you are in.

35

Put it into action

How to be more introvert

If you are an extrovert, you can practise being more introvert using these techniques:

- Allow yourself to be more reflective and thoughtful; keeping a diary will help you become more inward and spend time capturing your thoughts alone. This is not easy for an extrovert to do.
- Take up some solitary hobbies – painting, reading or walking will help you learn to be happy with your own company and only having yourself to speak with.
- Learn to pause and to be more patient; allow yourself to stop being in such a hurry to speak up, rush into something or share your latest idea.
- Become a very attentive listener; let yourself listen first and think before you start speaking. Stop always being the first one to speak up in a group discussion or meeting.

How to be more extrovert

If you are an introvert, here are some ideas for being more extrovert that you might find useful at home and work:

- Do not hide away; spend more time in other people's company. When you are with them, push yourself to speak more. Leave your office door or study door open. Invite people to connect with you more often – your colleagues at work or your neighbours at home.
- Be the one to speak up first in meetings and discussions; try speaking as thoughts come to you rather than inwardly reflecting first before speaking up.
- Leave your comfort zone; find social activities where you can practise expressing yourself. At one extreme you might choose to join a debating or toastmasters club where you would be compelled to speak and present in public.

LIVE WITH AN OPEN MIND

'There's an importance of keeping an open mind. The brain is programed to protect us, and that can mean imposing limits on what it thinks we can or should do. Constantly push at those limits, because the brain can be way too cautious.'

Chrissie Wellington

Are you really open-minded or do you only see what you have already observed and only hear what you have already listened to? We are creatures of habit and love things to be the way they were.

When you stubbornly stick to your opinions and conclusions, it's impossible to take in new information and ideas. Ignoring fresh perspectives and ways of seeing the world, or sweeping ideas we don't like under the carpet, closes us off and prevents us from growing to our full potential.

It's particularly true of our own lives that we often think we know with certainty the answers to the challenges and questions facing us: What am I doing? What should I do next? Where am I going? Whom should I connect with? What should I say? Why am I doing something and what do I want?... Sometimes we delude ourselves by posing questions when in our minds we already have the answer we want to hear. Successful people are always open-minded because it's only when you assess different options, ideas and decisions equally that you can make the right choices

Practise being open-minded. Learn to enjoy listening and taking in new ideas, information and opinions. Question views you've always had but never challenged. The alternative is to risk running on autopilot, stubbornly frozen in your old habits and thought patterns. No matter what choices and decisions you are facing, always do so with an open mind.

> When you stubbornly stick to your opinions and conclusions, it's impossible to take in new information and ideas.

36

Put it into action

Stop being stubborn

Ask those close to you if they see you as someone who is open to new ideas and opinions. Do you:

- listen well to others' points of view?
- take on board alternative suggestions and ideas?
- adjust your own thinking accordingly?
- let go of your strongly held opinions about how things should be done?

We can all be a little stubborn so don't worry if you are told you can be a little closed-minded at times. The goal of this exercise is to start being more conscious of yourself – to start observing when you are being closed-minded and clinging to ideas that may not be optimal for your success.

Next time you catch yourself arguing with someone simply to justify your own position, stop yourself and instead try to understand their different perspective.

An easy test of how closed-minded you are is how often you use the 'but' word. Look out for how often this crops up in your daily conversation. Every time you say it you might be closing yourself off to an alternative and valid idea. From now on, when you hear yourself about to say 'but', stop yourself and listen instead.

Welcome the opinion of others

Closed-mindedness can drive people away from you. People stop sharing with you and start holding back their opinions and ideas if it's clear you rarely listen or care about what they have to say.

A powerful tool for remaining open-minded is to always ask questions such as:

- 'What do you think?'
- 'What alternatives can you suggest?'
- 'Do you think I might be wrong in my thinking?'
- 'Do you think I am being too stubborn?'

BE THE BEST PARENT

'There are times as a parent when you realize that your job is not to be the parent you always imagined you'd be, the parent you always wished you had. Your job is to be the parent your child needs, given the particulars of his or her own life and nature.'

Ayelet Waldman

Sadly, most people I coach beat themselves up about how they have raised their children. They feel that their children are not enough of so many things – happy, emotional, sporty, diplomatic, bright, respectful, academic, friendly or ambitious. We seem to forget that a child is not a machine to be fixed or programmed. They are unique combinations of personality traits, experiences and understandings.

Parenting is a process of allowing the joys and wonders of having children in your life to overshadow any downsides. Too often I meet parents who cannot get over the shock of what having children has done to their lives! Sure, it's a shock leaving the world of couple-dom and suddenly being a family with all the responsibility, lack of spare cash and sleep that it involves. It can be very easy to become unhappy with the changes that parenthood brings.

There is a saying that only upon becoming a parent do we truly appreciate our own parents. Whatever your relationship with your own parents, you must forge your own path, working with your spouse to create your own rules. One look at the hundreds of books on parenting shows you that there is no one single list of golden rules to follow. Instead, there are themes you are encouraged to follow to help ensure that your children are nurtured in an optimal way. But at the end of the day you must have the confidence and patience to bring up your offspring in your own way, helping them blossom into adults capable of creating their own successful lives.

You must have the confidence and patience to bring up your offspring in your own way, helping them blossom into adults capable of creating their own successful lives.

37

Put it into action

Be a role model

Children see, record, learn and mirror everything around them. How you choose to be as a parent has a profound impact on them. In years to come do not be surprised at how your children have turned out, since much of what they are comes from copying you. You must always walk your talk, being conscious of being a role model. It stands to reason that:

- you cannot encourage your children to share when they see you being selfish
- your children may not grow up to be loving if you are constantly mean to their other parent.

If you have nothing good to say, then don't speak. Be careful of speaking badly about others in front of your children. If you are separated or divorced, never speak ill of your ex, who, after all, remains their parent.

The best advice I can give is to be yourself, trying to ensure that the 'yourself' you are being is someone that you would be proud of your children learning from and emulating.

Let your children discover themselves

Allow your children to discover their own passions, ambitions, dreams and beliefs. Read them fairy tales and encourage them to dream and be creative and to have wild imaginations. Allow your child's sense of wonder and possibility to blossom. Let their uniqueness flow. Be careful when encouraging them to take up certain activities and hobbies. Show them, encourage them but do not force them. Do not push them to partake in activities just because they are what you did as a child or wished you had done. Remember that life is about finding one's own path and solutions. Encourage them to solve problems themselves and to seek their own answers – teaching them to fish rather than always giving them fish on a plate. Learn to be more accepting and understanding of their own choices.

WALK AWAY FROM POLLUTION

'In an underdeveloped country don't drink the water. In a developed country
don't breathe the air.'

Jonathan Raban

Polluted environments are bad for your health, cause stress or make you unhappy. Whether it's man-made or natural, either way, steer clear of pollution.

I once considered moving to work and live in a new city. My wife and I spent a couple of days visiting schools and looking at houses there. The air pollution looked bad and our eyes stung and mouths tasted of pollution. Not surprisingly, we chose not to relocate there.

Uncomfortable pollution can be found everywhere across the world. Friends recently moved to London from a small town in Dorset. They were shocked by the city's constant noise and dirty air.

But it's not just about air quality. Pollution can take many forms and so often goes unnoticed until it is too late. You may have experienced:

- working in an office without any natural light or fresh air
- living next to a noisy motorway or railway line
- living in the middle of a city where you are forced to have blackout curtains to help you sleep
- having your garden back on to a smelly canal or refuse tip
- living in a lovely village where each year you suffer hay fever
- spending all day in a noisy office with music blaring out that you hate.

Learn to spot the signs and recognize how your environment affects your health and stress levels and, if necessary – get away.

Learn to spot the signs and recognize how your environment affects your health and stress levels…

38

Put it into action

Understand what is really making you uncomfortable

Everyone loves a bit of a moan. It's easy to adopt a 'don't blame me, blame them' kind of mentality. What you need to ask yourself is 'What am I really feeling uncomfortable or unhappy about?'

- Are you feeling stressed because of living with noise pollution or is your stress coming from having just moved to a new city?
- Is the poor visibility and air quality upsetting you because of its effects on your house price or its effects on your health?
- Are you feeling unhappy about the poor air quality or about your partner constantly complaining about the poor air quality?

Make small adjustments

You can always escape pollution. You can move house, change jobs, even move to a new country if you have to. Change what you can and accept what you cannot. If you choose to live and work in a city like London, New York, Beijing or Jakarta, then you really must accept that there is little you can do to improve the air quality. You may have to walk less outside or start wearing a face mask. Use air filters in your office. Filter the tap water at your home. Use an automated air freshener. Install double glazing in your bedroom. There are always choices.

Make a list of how pollution is bothering you and alongside every item note the smaller or larger changes and adjustments you can introduce to manage its effects.

LEAVE YOUR COMFORT ZONE

'I'm continually trying to make choices that put me against my own comfort zone. As long as you're uncomfortable, it means you're growing.'

Ashton Kutcher

If you have the perfect life with all the good fortune and success you desire, stay in your comfort zone. Do not be tempted out of it whatever you do. Otherwise be ready to step out of it now. Success will not come to *you*, you have to go and find it.

We all live within comfort zones. It's reassuring to know exactly where you are and what you do. It's nice that failure is not a big problem. What does your comfort zone look like? Are you:

- staying in your job and not pushing for a challenging promotion?
- staying in a relationship that seems OK, when in your heart you know you want out?
- holding back from starting a new business?
- putting off going back to university or starting dance classes?

Why do we get stuck in comfort zones? Why do we hold back from committing to things we know we really want to do? It comes down to fear of failure – we are terrified of things not going to plan, hearing the word 'no', or some other unspecified embarrassment.

So why does anyone ever leave their comfort zones? The most common reason is when the pain or cost of *not* changing becomes too much to bear – greater than the benefits of actually maintaining with the status quo.

Sometimes it is what we are missing out on, the so-called 'opportunity cost', that motivates us to make a change – when you want something so much that you are willing to step into the unknown to get it.

Success will not come to *you*, you have to go and find it.

39

Put it into action

Understand your fears and worries

Understanding your fears, anxieties and concerns can really help you move out of your comfort zone. What are the negative influences that play out and repeat themselves in your life? Ask yourself now: what do you most worry about and fear when faced with change? Is it:

- fear of losing money, prestige or other things?
- worry about what others will think and say?
- fear of failing, loss of face and being embarrassed?
- discomfort with the unknown and the unexpected?
- fear of losing what you have become used to, even if it is not ideal for you?

The pain is worth the gain

When a need to leave a comfort zone arrives and you find yourself saying 'I should really make a change' or 'I ought to seize this new opportunity', ask yourself two sets of questions and compare the benefits with any downsides:

- 'What would I gain by making the change?'
- 'What will I miss out on by staying where I am?'

The benefits are normally obvious and easy to explain. It might be a better work–life balance, an easier commute to work, improved relationships and so on.

- 'What is the cost or pain that I must face in making such a change?'
- 'What is the price of changing the status quo?'

This can be harder to formulate and so often boils down to your list of fears and worries. When coaching people around this comfort zone issue, I find it helpful to ask: 'What is the worst that can happen to you? How likely is this really to happen? Does such a worst-case scenario really need to hold you back from making a change that you agree you really want to or need to make?'

APPRECIATE THOSE CLOSEST TO YOU

'Make it a habit to tell people thank you. To express your appreciation, sincerely and without the expectation of anything in return. Truly appreciate those around you, and you'll soon find many others around you.'

Ralph Marston

Have you shown someone today that you really appreciate them? There are countless opportunities to show how grateful and thankful you are to those around you so make sure that you take them. Look out for the little things that people do – putting food on the table, giving up time to support you through a crisis, covering for you when you need time off.

It's easy to take these things for granted, especially when it becomes normal or repetitive. Failing to acknowledge, listen to and observe those with whom you live, work and spend your time is sadly all too common. As well as ignoring what they may be doing and saying, it is also possible that you will be ignoring their feelings.

Try not to fall into this trap. You might be tempted to blame your past – claiming 'But my parents never gave me thanks, praise or love.' Anyone can learn to do these things in any number of different ways. Sometimes just a few words are enough but it can be lovely to surprise someone with a card or present.

Have you shown someone today that you really appreciate them?

40

Put it into action

The key is to remember

Your challenge is to always remember to show your thanks and gratitude. People hate being forgotten and undervalued. Ask yourself on a daily basis 'Who do I need to appreciate today?' Keep a notebook to help you remember.

Rather as with a person's birthday or even your wedding anniversary, it is better to remember and acknowledge the day even if you have not planned an elaborate show of appreciation than to forget about it altogether. Do anything rather than nothing.

The question of how you show appreciation is normally easily decided once you are clear that you wish to appreciate someone at all.

Go beyond just saying thanks

Of course, it's important to say thanks, but it's not always enough. When thanks is said repetitively without feeling, it loses its power. For example, you might want to expand on a simple thank-you as follows: 'Thanks again for going to the effort of speaking with your boss about how I could switch departments. I do understand that you were not comfortable bringing up this topic for fear of showing undue favouritism. I really do appreciate that you were willing to ask.'

Showing authentic appreciation can be most impactful when it is least expected and when it acknowledges the effort that the other person has gone to.

SEEK WISDOM AND USE IT

'By three methods we may learn wisdom: First, by reflection, which is noblest; second, by imitation, which is easiest; and third by experience, which is the bitterest.'

Confucius

Discovering your inner guru doesn't mean being old and sitting about in a cave. If you are observant and reflective, you're already halfway there.

In fact, you might be unaware of just how much experience and knowledge you already have about the world around you. It's easy to take for granted but this experience, if you can tap into it, can benefit you in so many ways – helping you know what you want in life, what you love, what your strengths are, what and how you can do things, what you are afraid of, and so on. Tapping into this is an essential tool for having a successful life.

Wisdom is all around you. In addition to tapping into your own, make a point of seeking it out in others. You'll be surrounded by plenty of older people who have 'been there and done that', but equally don't ignore wisdom from unexpected sources like your children, nephews, grandchildren, whose thoughts and insight can be enlightening.

One of the main uses of wisdom is to enable you to grow as a person through becoming more self-aware and developing yourself. A sign of true wisdom is when a person takes responsibility for their life and resists the temptation to blame others for their situation. Your life is your responsibility. Accepting that is a sign of true wisdom and it involves asking yourself questions about yourself and what you must change. To paraphrase the words of the mystic Rumi, yesterday you were clever, so you wanted to change the world; today you are wise, so you are changing yourself.

A sign of true wisdom is when a person takes responsibility for their life…

41

Put it into action

Seek experiences to develop your wisdom

If you spend all your time doing or thinking the same things, you will eventually become an expert, but only in the same recurring situations. Once you have mastered the tasks you won't gain any new insights or lessons. There comes a time when you may need to move beyond what you have been doing in order to gain new experiences and insights.

There are lots of simple ways to make a habit of learning new things:

- When you're working out at the gym, try a different piece of equipment or routine.
- When you're at work, take on new tasks and responsibilities. This can lead to break-throughs in your understanding of business and how you approach things.
- In your free time, break the routine of how you spend your weekends and holidays. Throw yourself into a new road trip or taking on new hobbies.
- Break up even the most inconsequential of routines like what sort of tea you drink to instil the habit of trying something different.
- Spend more time learning from others – it might be your retired neighbour, your elderly grandparents, your children or an ex-boss. Your wisdom grows as you spend time discussing your dreams, challenges and concerns with a range of different people.

Allow yourself to better judge and discern

Get into the habit of coming up with your own answers to problems and situations you face on a daily basis rather than deferring to others. Next time you need a solution, don't ask 'What should I do?'; instead, share the problems and your ideas of how you will solve or approach it. Ask others to challenge your thinking, your understanding and your conclusions. Through really listening to what they have to say, and thinking through how you will respond, you will deepen your own wisdom.

MODEL THE BEST

'To achieve your goal you have to get into the character of a winner. Confident people have a certain way of presenting themselves. Observe people who are confident and successful and try to emulate them in your life.'

Dr Anil Kr Sinha

If you have a talent for being a copy-cat, it could just be the key to your success. By observing and learning from successful people, you can zoom up the learning curve and more easily achieve your goals.

Neuro-linguistic programming (NLP) works on the idea that you can quickly achieve a goal by replicating the behaviours and thought patterns of people who are already doing it successfully. The technical term is 'modelling', which fundamentally means copying or recreating what others are already doing well – whether it's at work, school or in sports.

Whatever your goals, it is likely that there's someone you could copy. The beauty of this technique is that there's really no limit to what you can use it for. It could be for losing weight, getting promoted, becoming a great public speaker, learning to pass exams or maintaining a long-term relationship.

It's done by observing, understanding and then copying the other person's behaviours, actions, thinking and communication style.

It involves understanding that our thoughts and actions are part conscious and part unconscious. The secret to success is to become both consciously and unconsciously competent in all aspects of a task or process and to understand that success depends as much on your verbal and non-verbal communication with both yourself and with others as on the things you choose to do. It is not enough to copy a great rower, carpenter, accountant or teacher if inside you are telling yourself you will never be as successful as them.

Modelling others is not enough in itself – it is only a stepping stone to your own success – but it is a powerful technique to have in your armoury.

And, in any event, you need to allow your own individuality, experiences and dreams to shine through to allow yourself to surpass the ones you have been imitating.

By observing and learning from successful people you can zoom up the learning curve and more easily achieve your goals.

42

Put it into action

Observing success

Decide who it is that you want to emulate and be clear on what is it that you want to copy.

Put yourself in their shoes, asking yourself what are they actually doing, how are they achieving this and what is driving or motivating them.

Be clear in your own mind what success means and how it is different from normal.

You can normally answer the 'what' and the 'how' by spending time with the person you're modelling, observing what they do and how they do it. It's not always possible or even necessary to connect with the individual but, if you do have that opportunity, ask them questions such as:

- 'Before starting how do you plan to do what you do?'
- 'What do you make sure that you do each time you perform?'
- 'In what ways did you struggle before becoming more successful?'
- 'What must I remember and do to be like you?'
- 'What do you do that is different from others?'

The challenging part is to understand the person's inner mindset, motivation, attitude and communication style. You might learn this from observation and from speaking to them but you can also infer conclusions from what you observe – for example, you might notice that they are thick-skinned and persistent, reflect thoroughly before starting a task, or always seek feedback from others. From observations such as these you can begin to build up a sense of their mindset that will help you decide which behaviours it is essential to replicate if you are going to emulate their success.

Replicating what you observe

Once you understand how another person is achieving success, your challenge is to replicate their actions and behaviours. How you do this will very much depend on what it is you are trying to achieve. Copying their visible actions may not be so hard – and, at worst, you may need time and the benefits of trial and error. The bigger challenge is to adopt the ideal mindset and inner thinking – to dispense with those unnecessary and negative thoughts that can hold you back.

HAVE THE COURAGE TO FAIL

'It is impossible to live without failing at something, unless you live so cautiously that you might as well not have lived at all, in which case you have failed by default.'

J. K. Rowling

When did you last fail at something? Or, perhaps more tellingly, when is the last time you held yourself back from doing something for fear of failure? Worrying about failure must rank as the number-one reason why we do not realize more of our dreams. I am tired of coaching people who are scared of having a go at making changes in their lives. I often ask them what they think is the worst thing that could happen, in changing careers, leaving a toxic relationship or undertaking whatever change they are envisaging. Their responses rarely justify their holding back.

Be careful of living too much of your life in your head. Too often, our fear of failing far exceeds any possible reality.

A key concern that can paralyse even the most ambitious person is potential loss of face. We are so preoccupied with what others might think that we avoid chasing our dreams. Here's something that might surprise you. People spend a lot less time thinking about you than you think. Learn to be comfortable with your choices and don't let the actual, or potential, noise of other people's opinions hold you back from doing what you need to do.

Recognize those moments when it's time to move forward. Think about how important the goal is to your life's direction. Decide how important the potential success is balanced against the risk of not being successful. There is a chorus of well-known figures who have all said words to the effect that it is better to have tried and failed than to have never tried at all. You will never succeed unless you try. When looking back at your life you will regret more the chances you didn't take than those that you did.

> Be careful of living too much of your life in your head.

43

Put it into action

Practise taking calculated risks

You can always find a reason not to do something. Risks are everywhere and anything you might do can result in failure. You probably know someone who avoids doing things that seem easy to you, like getting on a plane for fear of it crashing or speaking in public for fear of being ridiculed. We each have our own internal risk threshold.

To achieve new things and to change aspects of your life, you will need to stretch your tolerance levels and take more calculated risks – risks that previously you might have avoided or risks that are quite new as you move down unexplored paths.

It's time to push your internal barriers and patterns.

Seek sounding boards and role models

Make a list of people who have overcome obstacles and fears to succeed in their lives. These people are your 'mentors with courage' and you should seek them out. They can help you look at the options facing you and help you explore the pros and the cons. They will give you the confidence to take new and necessary risks. You might fail and need to try again in another way. That is the price you have to pay on the road to success.

ACCEPT YOURSELF

'Love yourself – accept yourself – forgive yourself – and be good to yourself, because without you the rest of us are without a source of many wonderful things.'

Leo F. Buscaglia

If you've ever said 'I hate myself!', you're not alone. We all seem to spend parts of our life taking pity on ourselves and beating ourselves up for things that we might have done or not done, things we might have said or not said.

Modern life doesn't make it any easier. It's too easy to compare yourself to others who seem to be living the dream:

- We feel worse about our weight and bodies thanks to all the beauty- and health-related adverts, magazine articles and photos of 'ideal people'.
- Relationship problems become magnified out of proportion by the availability of all kinds of advice and suggestions.
- Social-media postings make other people's lives seem so much better than ours, adding to our anxieties or unhappiness.

There's a lot of truth in the idea that ignorance is bliss. Only last week I was coaching someone who, through online job postings and salary comparisons, had realized that they were being underpaid for their work. He was so angry with himself for having spent five years in his role accepting his pay packet. I had to remind him that he really enjoyed his job, had not struggled financially and could now seek higher pay if he wanted. Stop comparing yourself to others and you might just realize that everything's OK.

Sadly, how you feel about yourself affects those around you. We tend to project or transfer what we are negatively feeling on to other people. It manifests itself in jealous, cynical, critical, angry or unloving behaviour – not traits you'll find successful people displaying.

Stop comparing yourself to others and you might just realize that everything's OK.

44

Put it into action

Accept your uniqueness

You are unique and you should never even try to be an exact copy of someone else. Stop worrying if you do not fit into a box. Like everyone else, you are a mix of strengths and weaknesses, so stop beating yourself up about what is 'wrong' with you.

Instead, start being grateful for what you have and how you are.

Today try to get out of comparing mode. You will never be happy with yourself while you're comparing yourself to others. There will always be someone who appears richer, happier, healthier, more beautiful or in a more perfect relationship.

Project positivity

You have bad days; we all do. Who hasn't left the fridge door open, forgotten to put petrol in the car, slipped over on the supermarket travelator or left a bag in a taxi.

No matter how bad you're feeling about yourself, do not project it on to other people. Sure, tell them your feelings and concerns, vent your anger and frustration, but don't hurt those around you. Don't be sharp, dismissive or cold. When you project positivity, your own negative feelings will subside. Projecting positivity cuts off the fuel that allows negativity to grow. Let your feelings subside and you will find yourself becoming OK with what has happened. This is what it means to truly accept and love yourself.

WATCH AND MANAGE
YOUR THOUGHTS

'As a single footstep will not make a path on the earth, so a single thought will not make a
pathway in the mind. To make a deep physical path, we walk again and again. To make a deep
mental path, we must think over and over the kind of thoughts we wish to dominate our lives.'

Henry David Thoreau

Whether you think you are successful or unsuccessful, you are equally correct. What you
think has a profound impact upon your life. An earlier chapter suggested being more mindful with the aim of quieting your thoughts. Thoughts have a habit of appearing from nowhere and catching you off guard, and, inevitably, one thought leads to another.

This is particularly so with thoughts that contain anxious and fearful ideas. Let's take a simple example. You are moving jobs and you start thinking about what your new colleagues
will think of you and whether or not they'll like you. You begin debating what you will say
to them. You start thinking about what you'll wear when you meet them. You wind yourself
up with anticipations so that when you do finally meet them you're so anxious that it's hard
to be your normal easy-going self. Result: your new colleagues find you a bit cold and quiet.
Somehow your thoughts have helped create exactly what you feared in the first place.

Your thoughts can literally alter your reality. They can act as drivers spurring you in different directions. Your mind is so powerful, it can think you into different states and condi-
tions – think that you are happy, sad or confident or that you like a certain person and you
will probably begin to feel happier, sadder, more confident and that you really do like that
certain person.

If you think you are successful or if you think you are not, then you are equally correct.

45

Put it into action

Consciously think positively

Given the impact and influence of the thoughts that pass through your head each day, it stands to reason that you need to create and focus on positive and/or helpful thoughts, on thoughts that will help you be successful.

This involves being more conscious of the thoughts that are coming to you. If it is not clear what you are thinking, take a moment to ask yourself, 'What am I actually thinking here? Are these thoughts helpful and useful?'

When having negative thoughts – thoughts around worries, anxieties and fear – acknowledge them and learn from them. Ask yourself why your mind is worrying about what it's focused on. Sometimes these thoughts need to be acted on but often they are simply noise that your ego is throwing at you – thoughts that you know don't represent what you really feel. In moments like these tell yourself something like, 'Yes, I hear my fears, but I am happy to move ahead with my own ideas.'

When attempting to move on from negative thoughts, it is really helpful to create positive thoughts to fill their space. Positive thoughts can become mantras that you repeat to yourself, drowning out the noise of all the other thoughts going on. For example, when facing a difficult conversation with your boss, teacher or future father/mother-in-law, focus your thinking on how you would like the conversation to go, on what you would like to achieve.

REMEMBER PEOPLE

> 'You can make more friends in two months by becoming interested in other people than you
> can in two years by trying to get other people interested in you.'
>
> Dale Carnegie

How good are you at remembering details and facts about people? Politicians such as George Osborne and Bill Clinton are renowned for their ability to remember tiny details years later. It's surprising and delightful when someone you haven't met for a long time shows that they remember you. It may seem insignificant but, if you remember people, they will remember you and that's essential if you want to be successful in life.

OK, so some people are blessed with photographic memories but the rest of us can do this too with a little work. Keep a notebook. Jot down the names and a few personal details of everyone you meet. If you're going to a party or work meeting and you know who's going to be there, you can quickly refresh your memory before you arrive.

Today with social media you can connect with more people than ever before. You might have thousands of connections on Facebook or LinkedIn, but how many do you really know? The psychologist Robin Dunbar suggests 150 people is the maximum number that humans can comfortably have as friends. For the rest – get your notebook ready.

…if you remember people, they will remember you…

46

Put it into action

Listen more

Your task for today is to spend your next conversation listening. That doesn't mean say-ing nothing; it means your role in the conversation is to ask questions and encourage the other person to share things about themselves. Look for things that truly matter to them. You will learn so much more about people when you try this and you will probably discover something about yourself, too.

Keeping in touch

With regard to that notebook you've started, for it to really be of any use you need to do something with it at the end of each day. Create some kind of directory or database for your contacts and the important details you want to remember about them, even if it's just simple stuff like their children's names, birthdays and so on. With work-related contacts you can collect name cards and write notes on the card itself. Often, you can anticipate when you'll see people again, a friend's annual New Year's party for example, so be sure to revisit your database in advance.

DISCOVER WHAT DRIVES YOU

'I'm driven! What drives you? Cause you ain't gonna go to class just to go to class, to hear somebody teach.'

Eric Thomas

So much of our behaviour is driven by the need to prove something, something that usually dates back to when we were young. The need might be hidden from view but it's often right there below the surface.

Needs seem to originate in a few predictable ways:

- Sole or eldest siblings often exhibit a strong need to excel, to win at all costs and to be the centre of attention.
- Younger siblings often need more parental approval and support, appear less ambitious and are less willing to move far from their nests.
- Some children are pushed by parents or teachers, seeking perfection and never being still.
- Others might have spent their childhoods in poverty where gifts and abundance were rarities and money had to be spent carefully.

You might have seen people so busy winning at all costs that they become cold and money-oriented, or people always playing the 'poor me' victim who prefer to stay in a damaging relationship or a job they hate rather than take a risk and move on.

What childhood experiences made you who you are today? This is not an easy question to answer but it's one that's important to think about. Childhood needs can easily consume the real you, leaving no space for you to develop the best version of yourself.

Give yourself the space to develop the best version of yourself.

47

Put it into action

What is actually driving you?

Time to own up and admit why you are the way you are. Think about what made you ambitious or laid back. Is it to do with your position in the family – as the older, younger or middle child – or are you still looking for pats on the back from your parents?

It doesn't matter what drives you, just as long as you have your eyes open. Understand your patterns of behaviour and the reasons behind them rather than blaming your past for how you are today.

Drop unhelpful drivers

If you are happy to be driven in the direction you're going, that's fine. However, if you're not, then, starting today, explore the real issues and be prepared to change what drives you. Your thinking might flow like this:

- You attribute your perfectionism to a very demanding parent and you've always worked longer hours than strictly necessary as a result. Now that you're a parent, though, you find yourself repeating history and becoming angry with your children over their rushed homework. Is it time to break the cycle and stop demanding perfection of yourself and those around you?
- You're the kind of person who never says 'no', forever taking on more and more commitments. You think it may be to do with being an overachieving single child, always keen to please your parents. Now, as you begin to feel the pressure, you're wondering how long can you keep this up before you collapse and burn out from exhaustion.

APPRECIATE WHAT YOU'VE GOT

'Be grateful for what you have and stop complaining – it bores everybody else, does you no good, and doesn't solve any problems.'

Zig Ziglar

The grass is always greener on the other side – until you start to appreciate what you've already got, that is. Longing for the next big thing, whether it's status or material possessions, only makes you unhappy and restless.

The secret is to be grateful for what you have. Pause for a moment to truly appreciate what you've got. You'll probably discover that you don't actually *need* anything else at all. How good does it feel to realize that you already have everything you need?

That doesn't mean that you shouldn't try to improve yourself but you should learn to be thankful for where you are today and what you have in life. If you can't be grateful for what you have today, what makes you think you'll be grateful for what you have tomorrow?

Don't compare yourself to other people. Nobody cares about your neighbours' children's grades or the size of their TV. Competing is like an arms race. You upgrade your car; someone else gets a better car. It's your move, unless you call time on the whole thing – which is exactly what you need to do to break the cycle.

> Don't compare yourself to other people.

48

Put it into action

Be happy for other people

A good way to eliminate the envy that lies behind the 'grass is greener' mentality is to be happy for other people's successes. Reach out to your friend who's just won an impressive promotion in her organization and celebrate with her. When you welcome in positive emotions, your whole being responds positively. Try this today on social media. Instead of ignoring or giving a grudging 'like' to some news one of your contacts is sharing, leave a comment to properly congratulate them in a genuine and authentic way. You will soon feel the benefit of this shift of attitude coming right back at you.

Fill your own glass

I recently heard someone say that the glass is neither half full nor half empty – it is always refillable. What a wonderful way of viewing life.

Sit down and list what you do have, what you have achieved and experienced. Focus on the liquid in your glass rather than on the empty space. And stop comparing the size of your glass to others'. For everyone you know who has more than you there are millions with less. The world is filled with people who would love your green grass.

Review your list and, once you are at peace with what you have, you will be in a good place to plan what's important for you next, not driven by envy but by your own positive goals for living life to the fullest.

MAKE PEACE WITH YOUR PARENTS

'Love your parents and treat them with loving care. For you will only know their value when you see their empty chair.'

Anonymous

You cannot live a healthy and successful life if you are not at peace with your parents. Parents get a hard time. Yes, it's true that you can choose your friends but you can't choose your parents; however, if you are a parent yourself, you will have realized that it's not easy. There are no black-and-white rules to follow or perfect ways to bring up children. If you're not a parent, take it from me and others around you. Once you are able to appreciate what your parents did, you will hopefully be able to let go of any negative feelings you may still be holding on to.

It is really healthy to accept that your parents know you well and hopefully love you unconditionally no matter what you do or become. Your parents can be your best mentors and advisors; they can discuss your problems, fears, hopes and concerns with your best interests at heart. Parents can be fantastic at seeing patterns in your life and helping you spot recurring themes that may have begun when you were just a child.

If you are willing to ask the right questions and listen, they can help remind you of your patterns – in your relationships with people, work or money, for example.

Parents can be fantastic at seeing patterns in your life and helping you spot recurring themes…

49

Put it into action

Clear the air

Let go of your nonsense and give your parents a break. So what if you feel they were too harsh with you or lied about something important. Forgive them.

Sometimes to have the most meaningful relationship with your parents you have to clear the air. Today is the day you talk to them about the thing you've been meaning to talk about but never do.

With your parents – in fact, with anyone close to you – it's essential not to sweat the small stuff and allow things to get out of proportion.

Give them your time

Listen to things from your parents' perspective. Would they like you to visit them more often, or stay a bit longer when you do? Would they just like to hear your voice more often? As I have become a parent of older children, I realize that all parents would like more time and attention from their kids. Enough is never enough.

Do not ask your parents 'How long do you want me to stay or how often should we speak?' Instead, ask yourself how much time and attention you are willing to give them. There are no hard-and-fast rules. Some people feel good speaking with their parents every day and others only once a month. Perhaps a less frequent but more meaningful conversation is better than regular short calls to simply ask 'How are you?' Find whatever works for you.

LAUGH MORE

'Laughter connects you with people. It's almost impossible to maintain any kind of distance or any sense of social hierarchy when you're just howling with laughter. Laughter is a force for democracy.'

John Cleese

Laughing and smiling can save your life. That might sound a little dramatic but studies of the effects of laughter reveal all kinds of health benefits, from lower blood pressure, reduced levels of the stress hormone cortisol, the release of happiness-creating endorphins and increased levels of an important antibody that fights bacteria and respiratory infections. There is even a study showing that repeated laughing or smiling actually burns calories.

Laughter is infectious, too. On YouTube you can watch experiments on the London Underground where a person starts laughing and giggling uncontrollably without pausing. Within minutes all of those around them have joined in without even knowing why the stranger is acting so happy. People are naturally drawn to those who are happier and more positive than others.

The bottom line is: laughing is good for you and it makes you popular, too. Seriously, for the good of your health, lighten up.

...laughing is good for you and it makes you popular, too.

50

Put it into action

Practice makes perfect

This is where you learn to laugh more. If you don't smile enough, then commit to change.

- Learn to be relaxed and positive with other people. Smile when listening to other people speak.
- Act positive even if you may not feel that way inside.
- Seek funny and entertaining breaks from your normal everyday routine.
- Watch a comedy at the cinema, read a book of jokes and seek out fun experiences and moments.

It's important that you identify the things that drain your happiness. For your own sake, spend less time with unhappy and depressing people and do not let their energy and attitude bring you down.

Be positive even when others are not

Be a pillar of positivity for all of those around you. If someone is depressed, be the one who lightens the mood by laughing or smiling.

Do not let convention hold you back from showing your happiness. Often, in quiet, stressed or formal situations people need someone to break the ice to allow them all to start relaxing, smiling and laughing.

STAY UNIQUE

> 'A note of caution: We can never achieve goals that envy sets for us. Looking at your friends
> and wishing you had what they had is a waste of precious energy. Because we are all unique,
> what makes another happy may do the opposite for you.'
>
> Marcus Buckingham

No two people are quite alike. Even identical twins have their own personalities, desires and ambitions. I love the words of the writer Jason Mason when he says, 'You were born an original. Don't die a copy.'

Trying to fit in can be necessary, useful and good. We often start practising it at school and in our families, and take it on into adulthood. It is there in many aspects of our adult lives – being like others in work meetings and discussions, dressing like friends, having similar opinions to our colleagues'.

But it's important to stand out from time to time too, especially if you are fitting in just to play it safe and avoid being questioned or challenged. If you're going to be true to yourself, there will be many moments in your life when – to paraphrase Sting – you have to be yourself no matter what they say. Successful people do this all the time. The skill is getting the balance between conforming and being open about your unique ambitions, personality traits, desires and strengths.

You have to be yourself no matter what they say.

51

Put it into action

What are your unique characteristics?

If I was your coach, I might spend time observing you and those you live, socialize and work with. What do you think I would observe? What combination of ambitions, desires, experiences, background and personality traits make up who you are? Make a list and give it two columns, one to tick if you truly live a particular trait and the other if you keep that trait hidden. What are you hiding away?

- Do you love animals but hide it because your parents or partner hates having pets at home?
- Do you want to live in the country with nature all around but live in the suburbs to be more convenient for work?
- Do you want to travel to wild untouched parts of the world, but always follow your friends on package holidays?

Look at your list and ask yourself: 'In what ways am I not being true to myself? What do I need to stop doing and whom do I need to stop copying?'

Stop chasing others' uniqueness

Why chase someone else's dreams; what's wrong with your own? We all have a unique set of needs, desires and ambitions but get caught up in other people's dreams about how to live.

Newsflash: it doesn't matter if you miss out on *other people's* aspirations and achievements – put your time and energy into chasing your own.

SLEEP WELL

'Your life is a reflection of how you sleep, and how you sleep is a reflection of your life.'

Dr Rafael Pelayo

According to the National Sleep Foundation, we are the only mammals that willingly delay falling asleep. If you were a dolphin or lion, you would simply fall asleep when tired, but humans choose to burn the midnight oil reading, working, playing – anything other than sleeping.

Sleep deprivation causes all kinds of problems. You lose sharpness, your concentration levels suffer, you feel grumpy and act negatively. Sustained lack of sleep can be very damaging to health – it weakens your immune system, leads to heart problems, kills your sex drive and increases your risk of diabetes.

And don't think your lie-in at the weekend is helping either. One researcher has shown that the Monday-morning blues is just your body struggling to cope with mild jet lag – your body is suddenly having to get used to a different sleeping pattern after a weekend of lounging in bed. So, if catching up with sleep at the weekend is out, what can you do?

Sleep deprivation causes all kinds of problems.

52

Put it into action

Don't take your worries to bed

Sleeping on a problem doesn't mean thinking about it until the very moment you fall asleep. It means that you'll come back to it tomorrow when you're fresh and focused. Taking your emails, worries and even conference calls to bed with you just guarantees a poor night's sleep. Your mission today is to switch off from your daily work and family challenges at least one hour before bedtime. You have a one-hour pre-bed moratorium on anything remotely stressful. Instead, read a book, listen to music, do some stretching exercises or sit on your balcony staring at the night sky if you want.

When asleep stay asleep

A good night's sleep ensures that you are fully alert and energized to face the day. Make sure that your phone is on silent and do whatever you can to minimize traffic noise and light – buy some blackout blinds, close the windows, and even switch rooms if you have to.

In the morning give yourself time to wake up. Set your alarm a few minutes earlier than you need to get up and use the extra time to stretch, drink water and slowly get up.

GO YOUR OWN WAY

> 'If we will be quiet and ready enough, we shall find compensation in every disappointment.'
> Henry David Thoreau

Disappointing people is part of finding your own way in life. There will never be a shortage of well-meaning people in your life, happy to advise you and create expectations about how you should be, act and do:

- 'You ought to study there as they have the best course for you.'
- 'Don't buy a house in that part of town.'
- 'Don't be a fool and resign now – your career prospects are so good.'

Sometimes taking advice makes sense but too often well-intentioned guidance is based on others' experiences and aspirations – not on a clear understanding of yours. Don't be surprised if the best way forward is to fly in the face of advice, even if it's advice from those close to you.

Ignoring advice can offend people, but the simple truth is that being true and authentic to yourself will always disappoint somebody out there. Those who truly love and care for you will not allow their disappointment to linger for long. Encourage them to understand and accept your decisions and choices by talking with them. Take heart from the words of Dr Seuss: 'Be who you are and say what you feel, because those who mind don't matter and those who matter don't mind.'

...being true and authentic to yourself will always disappoint somebody out there.

53

Put it into action

Guilt – get over it

Feeling guilty for doing the opposite to what someone close to you has suggested is natural. Most of us like to please people and it can be hard standing firm when you have a very insistent relative saying 'Choose A' when you want to choose B. Acknowledge the feeling of guilt. If it helps you, talk about it with the person you think you have disappointed. Explain why you made the choice you have made.

When you do disappoint somebody, reflect upon what you can learn from the situation. Often, your perception is wrong or exaggerated – the other party may not be as disappointed as you think or they might even be pleased you bucked the trend and chose your own path.

If it turns out that other people's advice might have been better to follow, be thick-skinned. Be ready for people to say 'I told you so.' We all make mistakes. Learn from what happened and move on.

Some people can never be pleased

Some people in your life may be impossible to please. They might act as if you are disappointing them no matter what you do. All you can do is learn to live around them. If it becomes unbearable, move on, spending less time in their company and stop sharing your plans, dreams and intentions with them.

SEEK SIMPLICITY

'Any intelligent fool can make things bigger, more complex, and more violent. It takes a touch
of genius ... and a lot of courage to move in the opposite direction.'

E. F. Schumacher

We live in a world where being constantly busy and on the go is the norm and where we are always expected to have ideas, arguments and opinions about everything. Our minds make us think that life needs to be more complicated than it really should be. Confucius put it so well: life is really simple, but we insist on making it complicated.

It can be a little embarrassing *not* to be busy and to feel no compulsion to keep up with everything that is going on. So people keep filling their days with things to do and goals to achieve – creating busyness and complexity to fill the gaps. Very few people when asked if they are busy at work would answer, 'No, not at all.'

At the same time we plan summer vacations where we dream of doing very little and thinking about even less. What a shame that we save up simplicity for only those two weeks a year in the sun.

Simplicity is the smart choice for successful people but it's not an easy choice. It takes bravery to find straightforward solutions and to de-clutter your time, your commitments and your life.

Simplicity is the smart choice for successful people...

54

Put it into action

Simplify your commitments

KISS, or 'Keep It Simple, Stupid', is a marvellous piece of advice. No matter what you are doing or saying, ask yourself 'Am I keeping this as straightforward as possible? Is this as clear, honest and to the point as needed?'

The easiest way of simplifying conversations, promises and commitments to other people is to be 100-per-cent honest and promise only what you will actually do. This one simple technique will instantly eradicate broken promises, delays, misunderstandings and arguments.

De-clutter your life

Think twice before acquiring something new and, when you do buy something, give something else away. Try letting go little by little. Start with one room at a time. Aim to create space that will remain empty. Have drawers that are clear of papers, garage shelves that are free from junk.

DO IT TODAY

> 'Life hangs on a very thin thread and the cancer of time is complacency. If you are going to do something, do it now. Tomorrow is too late.'
>
> Pete Goss

Delay and procrastination are the most common success killers – if you are happy to fail in any aspect of your life, start by avoiding doing today what needs to be done.

Many of the leaders that I coach suffer from procrastination and we spend time exploring the related questions 'Why not start now?' and 'If not now, what is the price you will have to pay?' The question over the price of not starting now is key. If you do not spend time now on an important task, could you be leaving yourself a mountain to climb when you do eventually start. At that time you will probably have new and other urgent tasks to work on. This can equally apply at home, school, in your social life as well as at work.

- Delaying having an important conversation can destroy relationships. Are you avoiding apologizing for a mistake you have made?
- Not starting an exercise or diet regime today can seem a zero-impact decision. But what about if you also delay tomorrow or the day after.

Christopher Parker put it so well when he stated that procrastination is like a credit card: it's a lot of fun until you get the bill.

…if you are happy to fail in any aspect of your life, start by avoiding doing today what needs to be done.

55

Put it into action

Be honest with yourself

Ask what is stopping you from doing something:

- Is it laziness on your part or do you do things at the last minute only when your back is against the wall?
- Do you not really feel the task is important and cannot motivate yourself to get started?
- Are you unsure how to complete the task or what to do first?
- Are you afraid of failing and the embarrassment that would follow?

Start small

- Today push yourself to start something that you've been putting off.
- Break the task down into manageable bite-size pieces so that it seems more achievable; after all, even mammoth tasks are just made up of a series of small steps.
- Decide how many steps you can achieve today.
- Give yourself a goal for tomorrow and the next day.
- Start.

If in doubt...

Whatever your reasoning for procrastinating, ask yourself which is worse:

1 dealing with the momentary discomfort, anxiety and stress that comes with biting the bullet and starting; *or*

2 dealing with the fallout of delaying doing something including the impact on your reputation, credibility and trustworthiness – and the impact on others who are waiting for you to do something?

In other words, is it really worth putting off until tomorrow what you can do today? If in doubt, start now.

SEEK EXPERIENCES OVER THINGS

'Buy experiences, not things. Spending on experiences makes people happier than spending on things. Things get broken and go out of style. Experiences get better every time you talk about them.'

Jean Chatzky

Which do you remember better – going on your favourite holiday or buying your most treasured gadget? Chances are your memories of the trip are stronger. Ground-breaking research by Thomas Gilovich at Cornell University clearly shows that experiences bring more enduring happiness and fulfilment than material possessions.

Getting away, visiting a museum or taking a class can have a powerful effect on your satisfaction with life, sense of fulfilment, wellbeing and wisdom. Surprisingly, even experiences that go wrong give us positive memories and feelings – whether you lost your luggage in Greece, got an upset tummy in France, or sat through a disappointing Broadway musical. All these memories stay with us and live for ever.

Buying things gives a short-term buzz by comparison and when something you've bought goes wrong, who honestly has positive feelings about it? Worse still, things become dated and after a few weeks or months there'll be a better brand or style on the block.

I recently read a lovely anonymous quote that very much sums up the value of buying experiences: '"I regret spending money on that epic, life-changing trip" ... said no one, ever.'

Experiences bring enduring happiness and fulfilment.

56

Put it into action

Seek wide-ranging experiences

There are two groups of experiences:

1 those in which you participate, such as doing charity or voluntary work, playing sports, doing some form of art or drama, going on treks, taking classes such as cookery or writing

2 those where you watch and enjoy, such as going to the theatre or visiting a stately home or museum.

Try to get a mix of both where you can. Do not let money be something that stops you seeking experiences at any point in your life. Remember that many museums and exhibitions are free as is walking around new cities or in the countryside.

On your next holiday, why not build in something really rewarding, like some local charity work or a language course?

Put your camera away

Use your digital camera to briefly capture what you are experiencing rather than staring through your lens the whole time. If you're sitting on the hill next to the Acropolis, then just sit on the hill next to the Acropolis. Experience the view live. Photos will help you relive it and are fun to share, but experiencing the moment is what imprints it on your memory and you don't get that from a photo. Take a few pictures, then put your camera away.

HAVE CLEARLY WRITTEN GOALS

'If you have a goal, write it down. If you do not write it down, you do not have a goal – you have a wish.'

Steve Maraboli

The seemingly impossible dream can become reality with the help of a clearly written goal. In 1961 US President John F. Kennedy expressed his desire to put a man on the Moon before the end of the decade. It became NASA's written goal and target and the rest is history. In July 1969, only five months shy of that 'end of the decade' target, Neil Armstrong set foot safely on the Moon.

When is the last time you thought through and wrote down your goals and plans, turning your own 'Moon landing' dream into a doable action? Writing down your goals greatly increases your chances of achieving them. Numerous studies confirm this, including one at California's Dominican University which showed a 42-per-cent increase in success rate when goals are written down.

It is not enough to simply write down your dream and call it a goal. Being as detailed as possible can help you in a number of ways:

- It forces you to be clear about what you really want to achieve.
- It makes your goals memorable.
- It means you can produce action plans that will motivate you to work towards their achievement.

Writing down that you want to qualify as an accountant within 18 months, pass all your exams first time, and become a finance controller within your company within three years, is a lot more helpful than simply saying you would love to become a finance manager one day.

Dream can become reality with the help of a clearly written goal.

57

Put it into action

Keep a goals journal

Sir Richard Branson is a big fan of writing down goals. In a blog post referring to 2016 New Year resolutions, he advises readers to always carry a notebook to capture all of your ideas and goals. So many of Richard's many successes would not have happened had he not been such a big believer in writing down his goals.

So commit your goals to paper. Starting today, write down or type up the different range of things you want to achieve and do. Keep them in a diary, on your phone or on index cards. It does not matter where you write them – just make the effort to write them down.

Your written goals might start out as fluffy-sounding dreams ('I want to live in a big house', 'I want to retire early', 'I want to remain healthy'). That is OK. They are first drafts. Now expand upon each goal by asking yourself the following: Is it...

- Specific and clear enough?
- Measurable so that you will know when it is achieved?
- Attainable – and, if not, how can you make it attainable?
- Realistic and relevant to your circumstances and life?
- Timeframe bound with a clearly stated 'achieve by' date?

The majority of people are not this systematic in creating 'smart goals', a term attributed to the coach Sir John Whitmore. Is it any surprise that most people fail to reach them!

Make sure that you keep copies of your goals to refer back to later. They can serve as an anchor or compass. You can always update and change them, but first reflect on what the younger version of you had written. You might be surprised to realize that your past goals are as relevant today as they were when you wrote them.

Creating goals with others such as your partner, children or colleagues is also a good idea. You can write and discuss them together, helping one another plan how to achieve them. Share goals you have written by yourself selectively – only with people you trust or from whom you would like mentoring support and advice.

GIVE READING YOUR FULL ATTENTION

'How my life has been brought to undiscovered lands, and how much richer it gets – all from words printed on a page… How a book can have 560 pages, but in only three pages change the reader's life.'

Emoke B'Racz

According to statistics from Pew Research Center and the UK Government, only 55 per cent of Americans and 65 per cent of the British read books for pleasure. It's hard to imagine anyone who chooses not to read leading a genuinely successful life. Reading broadens your understanding and appreciation of life and of yourself. Oscar Wilde summed it up well when he said that it is what you read when you don't have to that determines what you will be when you can't help it.

It really does not matter whether you read fiction or non-fiction. It might be good to read longer stories once in a while, but I think reading short books, newspapers, magazines and blogs are all fine. What matters is that you seek out writing that feeds your mind and soul, giving you inspiring and uplifting thoughts, insights and information. Reading helps you see a bigger world of possibilities through other people's experiences, both in real life and fiction. It gives you new vantage points from which to view your own life.

Reading in your field of study or work allows you to have richer conversations and debates with others and helps you keep up to date on the latest thinking and ideas. This in turn allows you to participate more fully in decision-making and creative brainstorming.

Put simply, reading gives you a broader and deeper understanding of things.

…reading gives you a broader and deeper understanding of things.

58

Put it into action

Go deeper

Avoid only skim-reading and scanning things quickly. This happens too easily when you use your smartphone to browse social-media articles or news pages. Instead, allow yourself to read an entire magazine and book. Reading something in its entirety gives your mind time to absorb and to reflect upon what you have read.

Personalize your reading

Read things that suit your personal and peculiar tastes, interests and passions. Do not be lazy and simply buy from a bookshop's bestseller section. If you really want to excel and be successful, be ready to take a different path. Your challenge for today is to wander aimlessly around a bookshop seeing what books catch your eye. The author Haruki Murakami put it well when he said that, if you read only the books that everyone else is reading, you can only think what everyone else is thinking.

Join a book club or discussion group

Find like-minded readers and allow yourselves to explore the books together. The group might read the latest fiction or perhaps focus on particular categories of non-fiction such as nature, business or astronomy.

Turn from reading to writing

Finally, if you feel you have something to say, then start writing. Turn your own ideas, stories or theories into blog posts, articles or a book. Write the book that you have been dreaming of for years or that just came to you in the shower. Self-publish or seek a publisher and perhaps you will discover great fulfilment and even possibly fame as a new author.

GET A THICK SKIN

'Don't Take Anything Personally. Nothing others do is because of you. What others say and do is a projection of their own reality, their own dream. When you are immune to the opinions and actions of others, you won't be the victim of needless suffering.'

Don Miguel Ruiz

If you're easily offended, you're going to struggle on the road to success. Fact is, you have to have a bit of a thick skin just to get through the average day because, by accident or design, people can be quite hurtful. You might get overlooked on a party invite list, blanked in the street or someone may drop a clanger like 'Have you put on weight since we last met?'

It's not easy to keep it together in the face of things like this but, if you take everything said and done too personally, you could end up having no friends left at all. The most important thing to bear in mind is that whatever people do and say tends to be more about them than it is about you. The quote above nails this better than I ever could: what we say and do in life is a reflection of ourselves – we transfer our own feelings and beliefs on to the people around us.

When someone is at peace inside themselves it is usually projected in how they interact with others and treat other people. They will often come across as empathic, calm and understanding. Conversely, when someone is angry or bitter with their own life they can be cold and mean in their communication with those closest to them.

So next time something hurtful happens, better to take pity than to take offence.

It is better to take pity than to take offence.

59

Put it into action

Like water off a duck's back

If someone offends you, whether intentionally or not, try not to show your feelings. Hopefully, you won't have any occasion today to practise this, but your task, in preparation for when it does happen, is to get into a conscious habit of not responding to offence. Your reaction in future should be as follows:

1 Count to ten.

2 Smile.

3 Walk away.

It should be like water off a duck's back to you. Calmly let it go and move on. By all means remember that someone has affronted you, but don't take visible offence.

Sometimes you must speak up

There may be moments when you do need to respond; perhaps if someone has offended those around you – your team at work or your family. In that case, respond in a calm and mature way, simply by expressing what you see or hear. Ask the other person for clarification and whether they intended to be rude or offensive. If necessary, ask them to apologize.

Kick toxic people away

You cannot control what other people say or do but you can always walk away. Be ready to give the benefit of the doubt or have a calm word, but equally be ready to walk away from repeat offenders.

BE GENEROUS

'Obviously, you would give your life for your children, or give them the last biscuit on the plate. But to me, the trick in life is to take that sense of generosity between kin, make it apply to the extended family and to your neighbour, your village and beyond.'

Tom Stoppard

Surveys confirm that nearly all of us give our time for free or money to the less fortunate. Congratulate yourself – statistically speaking, you are probably already generous.

So, if being baseline generous is the new normal, what does the next step look like? Real generosity isn't just giving a couple of coins to a homeless person; it's stopping to talk with him, asking him how he is and trying to understand his situation, maybe offering to buy him some food or help in some other way. Occasionally, videos go viral on YouTube showing people literally giving the shirt off their back to help a homeless person keep warm. That's what real success looks like – being the person who gives without thinking about themselves to help others.

Generosity isn't all about money and time, either. Remembering to thank people, writing a glowing review or report – when you don't have to – these are the things that set truly generous people apart. And doing it without any expectation of return, too. Real generosity does not expect or seek repayment. As John Bunyan said: 'You have not lived until you have done something for someone who can never repay you.'

That's what real success looks like – being the person who gives without thinking about themselves to help others.

60

Put it into action

Start small

Look for ways to be generous. Really go out of your way to do the little things that are even more valuable because they're so unexpected:

- Give up your seat on the bus.
- Call your partner and tell them you have organized a weekend getaway (do not forget to organize it).
- Offer to look after your neighbour's house and feed the cat while they're away.
- Leave work early to watch your children's soccer match or dance recital.
- Know the birthdays of your colleagues, and surprise them by organizing an unexpected birthday celebration.
- Spend extra time with colleagues who might be struggling with their work or in need of a helping hand.

Acknowledge the generosity of others

When you observe others being kind and generous, often as unsung heroes not acting in hope of reward, be ready to thank them. You might simply go up to them to acknowledge their actions. Alternatively, you might publicly thank them, giving their name or simply leaving them unnamed. I sometimes do this on social media, posting comments such as 'Today I saw the owner of downtown coffee shop giving complimentary coffees and bagels to a couple of homeless men. What lovely generosity by an unsung hero.' I challenge you to share the next example of generosity that you observe today.

EAT AND DRINK WELL

'The only way to keep your health is to eat what you don't want, drink what you don't like, and do what you'd rather not.'

Mark Twain

All is not well on the food and drinks front. All around us we see evidence of eating and drinking problems. In the West at least, obesity, eating disorders and diabetes are all on the increase. Fast food and processed food consumption is becoming too common as people look for quick and cheap options. It's hard to claim to be having a successful life when you're ill with diabetes, heart disease or colon cancer.

The trouble is, it's hard to know what to believe or do as there's so much conflicting advice around. A multitude of health studies tell us what is and isn't healthy and it seems to change from one week to the next – whether it's about caffeine, protein or red wine.

If you're still young and carefree, does it even matter? Well, one thing is for sure – you will pay the price down the line if today you fill yourself with sugary drinks, fast food, processed food and alcohol. Most people can at least agree on this: you will age faster, weaken your immune system and die younger than if you look after yourself.

There are always going to be people who choose the instant rewards of carefree consumption over the delayed gratification of a longer and healthier life. Choose carefully – you don't get a second chance.

It's hard to claim to be having a successful life when you're ill with diabetes, heart disease or colon cancer.

61

Put it into action

All in moderation

Assuming that eating and drinking only healthy food is out of the question, the secret is to consume everything in moderation. If possible, avoid food and drinks that are clearly unhealthy or restrict yourself to only having them when you're out. At home, avoid fatty and sugary products.

Whatever you consume, avoid too much of any one thing and definitely avoid unhealthy binging. Over time the ideal is to narrow the gap between what you crave and what your body really needs.

Adopt some new habits

Before doctors diagnose something like gluten or lactose intolerance or even diabetes, proactively develop some healthy eating and drinking habits. You can do this quite simply by adopting the following approaches:

- Drink water first thing in the morning.
- Always have something for breakfast.
- Eat fresh fruit or mixed nuts when you feel like a snack between meals.
- Don't put sugar in hot drinks.
- Say 'no' to second helpings.
- Stop eating in the early evening, giving your food time to digest before you go to bed.
- Reduce your unhealthy habits – perhaps introduce a 'chocolate and wine at weekends only' rule.
- Cut out or reduce meats and dairy products – try to become a partial vegetarian or vegan.

SEEK AND CREATE HARMONY

'If life isn't about human beings and living in harmony, then I don't know what it's about.'
Orlando Bloom

You compose your own life. It's as if you are a piece of music and anybody near you can tell if it's playing in harmony. When it's out of tune, it can be so painful that other people will want to cover their ears! You need to be in harmony with yourself, with others and with the world at large.

When you are in harmony with yourself, four things are aligned: what you do, what you think, what you say and what you feel. In these moments, things flow without a sense of agitation, stress or tension. In some sense, your pieces all fit together and you feel less anxiety, stress, upset and guilt.

Being in harmony with others is all about being honest, walking your talk, being open, trusting and kind. The opposite is breaking promises, confrontation, misunderstanding and a lack of authenticity.

Being in harmony with the world at large takes many forms such as living sustainably and with nature, not against it. It might entail you working to stop a local nature reserve being turned into an industrial park or helping a group of refugees who are being resettled in your area.

It is hard to be at peace with things and people around you when you yourself are not at peace. As the Roman philosopher emperor Marcus Aurelius put it, 'He who lives in harmony with himself lives in harmony with the universe.'

Sadly, too many people never experience any sustained harmony in their lives.

You compose your own life.

62

Put it into action

Be in alignment

My advice is very simple: what you say, think, feel and do should be in alignment.

- When you want to lose weight, then go on a diet and exercise.
- If you promise to help someone, then remember to do it.
- If you feel sad and depressed, stop acting as if you are 100-per-cent OK.
- If you think someone is being unkind and mean to you, stop pretending that all is well between the two of you.
- If you don't want to stop smoking, then stop going through the motions – it will never work unless you mean it.

Don't say one thing, feel another, think something else and do the opposite!

The gain is worth the pain

In reality, this is one of the hardest challenges of all and you will need to delve into all 100 chapters of this book to aid you. It will be stressful and hard for you in the short term. You will probably upset people when you share what you really think or feel or when you stop doing something that you really no longer wish to do.

The longer-term benefit is that you start being more authentic and honest. Some people may pull away from you. If you do this, you can expect to have more honest and open relationships and friendships.

GET HOME ON TIME

According to a 2014 Ernst & Young global survey, one in three working people said that it had become more difficult to manage their work–life balance during the previous five years. I regularly coach individuals who complain of not being able to leave work until late at night. Thanks to constant cost saving, restructuring and streamlining, many of us are being asked to do more at work with the help of fewer colleagues. How can you hope to get home in time for dinner when you have double the amount of work to complete?

There seem to be two potential responses to rising workloads. You can either:

1 push back, trying to have the work given to others or not completed at all, or

2 work the extra hours.

If you refuse to take on the extra tasks, you risk putting yourself in the firing line when the next wave of restructuring hits.

Then there's peer pressure to take into account. It's easy to feel pressured to stay on at work beyond your normal finishing time, even when there is nothing urgent to do, simply because you don't want to be first to put their coat on.

The ideal is to achieve everything within your normal hours, making overtime an exception not a rule. This can be done and here you're going to learn how.

The ideal is to achieve everything within your normal hours…

63

Put it into action

Work smart

The secret is working smart. This does not mean working twice as fast or rushing every-thing. It is about doing what needs to be done as productively, creatively and efficiently as possible:

- Communicate your intention to others. If you need to leave the office at 5:30 p.m., let your colleagues know that's your plan. This subtly gives them the encouragement to do the same.
- Plan your working day well by mapping out what really needs completing today, how it will be done and by whom.
- Be ready to delegate work (including to your boss) and to push back on requests and tasks that you know are not important, essential or part of your area of expertise. This is where judgement is key – there will be times when you have to accept extra requests and go the extra mile.
- Stop wasting time procrastinating or doing unimportant tasks. If you spend an hour a day not being productive, you can't complain that you're always an hour late leaving the office.
- Imagine you are the laziest person in the world. Lazy people are great because they always find the easiest way to do things. Bill Gates said that he liked to hire lazy people for exactly this reason. So how would a lazy person tackle your to-do list?
- Encouraging your colleagues to work smart, too – it's a win–win because, if everyone's works smart, it will create a smart working environment or culture.
- Leave work where it belongs – at work. This includes all those worries, pressures and concerns that are churning around inside your head.

WORK FOR AS LONG AS YOU CAN

> 'It seems, in fact, as though the second half of a man's life is made up of nothing but the habits he has accumulated during the first half.'
>
> Fyodor Dostoyevsky

Retirement can kill you. According to a study by the Swiss economist Josef Zweimüller, every extra year of early retirement takes about two months off your life expectancy. If you're saving up your good times till you retire, it may be too late. Try to live a more stress-free, relaxed, healthy life now so that you will be able to enjoy it later when you retire.

There is a lovely French proverb that says that we spend the first half of life in longing for the second and the second half regretting the first. I think the secret lies in our expectations. I recently met with a group of retirees and asked them what advice they would give younger versions of themselves to ensure they had the best possible life after retirement. There were three common answers:

- Keep healthier by exercising well and consuming food and drink sensibly.
- Travel more and don't leave too much of your bucket list to complete when you're retired. It is better to have memories when older than unfulfilled dreams when younger.
- Don't rush to retire but let it happen gradually. Ease into it by going semi-retired or part-time rather than simply stopping work one day.

Retirement can kill you.

64

Put it into action

Be the person today you want be in retirement

All the evidence supports easing into retirement rather than planning to become a different person when you stop working. Ideally, you should create such a great life that you never need to consider retiring. But for salaried employees this can be hard – you have to officially stop at a certain age.

For today look for ways to act as if you have retired:

- De-stress and relax.
- Don't complain about being too busy or having nothing to do.
- Just be OK with what is in front of you.
- Find time for activities and hobbies.

I recently met a retired friend who had always planned that in his retirement he'd play golf every day. A year into it and he realized golf was making his life mundane and boring. He'd spent years visualizing the second half of his life only to find that he didn't enjoy what he'd been dreaming of.

HAVE GREAT BODY LANGUAGE

> 'Body language is a very powerful tool. We had body language before we had speech, and apparently, 80 per cent of what you understand in a conversation is read through the body, not the words.'
>
> Deborah Bull

Like it or not, your body language is visible 100 per cent of the time, sending out messages to others when you have no idea you are communicating and even less idea what you are actually saying. The writer Jarod Kintz put it well when he said, 'I love body language, because I can speak it without talking, without listening, and while my back is turned.'

To be successful in any area of your life, you need to be able to get on well with people and that means controlling the non-verbal messages you're giving out, as well as understanding the non-verbal messages you're getting back. Your body language needs to work with you in creating and maintaining good relationships. It needs to be the body language of success.

When you want to show that you trust others your body language has to back up the words you're saying. If you keep your arms folded and avoid eye contact, it'll contradict the message you're trying to give out. Other people may not pick it up at a conscious level, but unconsciously they could be affected by your body language – finding you cold or shifty thanks to that disconnect between your verbal and non-verbal communication.

Control the non-verbal messages you're giving out.

65

Put it into action

First impressions are everything

The most important moment to consciously manage your body language is when you first meet somebody. First impressions count, and it's true that you don't often get a second chance to make a first impression.

The secret is to exude confidence and trustworthiness:

- Always smile, make eye contact and have a firm handshake when first meeting someone (although you should be aware that this isn't appropriate in every culture).
- Have an upright posture whether you're standing or sitting. If you are sitting down, keep your legs together and don't fidget or move around too much.
- Dress appropriately for the occasion. If in doubt, dress more formally than you might normally – it is always easier to dress down than it is to do the opposite.

Deal with your bad habits

It's very hard to know what other people think of what your body language and non-verbal signals are saying to them. If you really have no idea, ask your friends or family and tell them to be honest with you. Better that they give you the unvarnished truth than that you fail a job interview or crash and burn on a date.

CHOOSE YOUR FRIENDS WISELY

'In life you'll realize that there is a purpose for everyone you meet. Some will test you, some will use you, and some will teach you. But most importantly … some will bring out the best in you.'

Anonymous

There is a saying that 'we are our five best friends' and it is true. The people you choose as your friends can have a major impact on you in both a positive and negative way.

Friends can strengthen and improve you or bring you down. Spend any amount of time with the same people and their habits will start to rub off on you. Things that would once have been unacceptable can easily become acceptable.

- A 2013 study published in the journal *Psychological Science* showed that having strong-willed friends can increase your own self-control. It is as if being in their presence boosts your own willpower.
- According to a 2014 study in the *Journal of Consumer Research*, when friends make poor or inappropriate choices, over time you are likely to copy and be dragged down by them.

When I coach clients I tell them that one of the best ways to understand themselves is to talk about their best friends and friends from their past they're no longer in touch with. Unlike with family members, you're normally free to choose your friends so you can observe patterns of long-term friendships.

The ideal is to have friends who bring out the best in you, help you grow and will always stand by you.

…have friends who bring out the best in you, help you grow and will always stand by you.

66

Put it into action

Make brave choices

I believe that everyone we meet, we meet for a reason. Sadly, we rarely know the reasons. Just because you have met someone new does not mean they must become or remain your friend. Be ready and willing to lose friends and acquaintances who repeatedly cause you pain or discomfort. Look out for people who:

- are mean and unkind to you
- belittle you and are jealous of you
- are selfish and even narcissistic
- have values, views or behaviours that make you uncomfortable.

You don't have to justify why you are moving away from them. You might want to share your concerns with them but don't expect them to change. People are often blind to their own weaknesses and may refuse to accept what you say or blame you for breaking up the friendship. Be ready for a challenge if you share mutual friends. Your pulling away may have an impact on the group dynamics. Be honest with those around you about your feelings and actions. Remain true to yourself.

Keep your real friends

It is sad when friends move away from us – over time or through circumstances like redundancy, illness or divorce. Often, it is the major life events that show you who your real friends are. These are the ones you should treasure.

BE CURIOUS

'We keep moving forward, opening new doors, and doing new things, because we're curious and curiosity keeps leading us down new paths.'

Walt Disney

Curiosity is an essential mindset in today's world. It is all about asking questions, exploring and being open to what's around you. It's about asking why things are the way they are. By doing this, you give your life more meaning and value. It is all about being open and not jumping to conclusions or being judgemental.

We are all born curious – you need only watch a baby exploring its surroundings to see this. Schooling and parenting can encourage natural curiosity to blossom or to wilt. Experts talk of leaving children to ask their own questions and to find their own answers – of becoming curious explorers. Sadly, too many young adults enter working life waiting and wanting to be given answers and solutions.

Curiosity needs to be rekindled and grown if you are to succeed in life. You need to rediscover that inner child, that curious explorer, who asks:

- 'How can I make this simpler, faster, more beautiful or cheaper?'
- 'How can I solve this problem in a new way?'
- 'How can I make this service more fun and enjoyable?'
- 'How can I integrate this cool Japanese idea into my design?'
- 'How can I make this appeal globally?'

> Curiosity is an essential mindset in today's world.

67

Put it into action

Be an expert questioner

Don't rush to find answers. Daniel Willingham, a cognitive scientist, says we are 'so eager to get to the answer that we do not devote sufficient time to developing the question'. Curiosity helps you ask the questions that produce better answers than you'll ever get from a quick scan of Google. Curiosity builds knowledge that bypasses simple conclusions and easy explanations.

Goodbye boredom

Train yourself to stay engaged with your surroundings, even if you feel the urge to switch off. Do not confuse boredom with a lapse in concentration. It is normal and OK for your concentration level to drop in a meeting or even at a social gathering. Take a short break to stretch or grab a coffee. When you get back, resolve to stay engaged. View any event or discussion as something to explore, learn from and make things better:

- What can you observe that others are all missing?
- How can you make the discussion more interesting?
- What can you learn about people around you just by watching them?

DO WHAT YOU SAY

'Sometimes people don't understand the promises they're making when they make them.'
John Green, *The Fault in Our Stars*

You should always be true to your word. When you do what you say you're going to do, you become the ultimate example of trustworthiness and trust is a very valuable commodity in life. In fact, I am beginning to think it's the most important quality you can have. It takes time to build up and just one rash moment or poor decision can wipe it all out.

Every day is full of small moments that put your word to the test – from promising to post the mail to buying milk on the way home. We all forget things once in a while but repeatedly overlooking the small tasks erodes trust over time.

The bigger challenge comes with life's larger promises and commitments where one breach can destroy all confidence – an affair, for example, or failing to complete a client tender proposal on time, which costs your company the business.

These moments can set back your plans for a successful life.

You should always be true to your word.

68

Put it into action

Do not agree it in the first place

Never agree to do something when you know you won't be able do it. Abraham Lincoln hit the nail on the head when he said we must not promise what we ought not, lest we be called on to perform what we cannot. If you are not sure, then say so. It is always better to disappoint by saying no beforehand rather than later by not performing as expected.

Take extra care with those special promises

Hold your important relationships sacred. These will probably be those with your partner, children, parents, close friends, bosses and key work colleagues. Take extra care with those who are part of your life on a daily basis. Always try to understand and remember the promises and agreements you make with those closest to you.

Most importantly, always take extra care of promises and commitments you make or should make with your better half.

PAUSE BEFORE YOU PRESS 'SEND'

'Compare sending someone a text message and getting a love letter delivered by carrier pigeon. No contest.'

Bryan Callen

Our entire working and social lives revolve around billions of emails, SMSs and Internet messages being sent between us all. We write them while eating, driving, running, in meetings or in the bathroom – is it any surprise that so many are sent that are wrong or inappropriate? No wonder at least one email provider has a 'Call back' button where you can 'un-send' an email just after you have pressed the 'Send' button.

I have coached many executives who have faced a variety of email and communication challenges. One would never read emails properly, another wrote long, vague messages that confused colleagues and another only wrote emails containing one-line messages that come across as cold and uncaring.

It's easy to forget that it's only relatively recently that communication moved online and mobile. We're all on a steep learning curve. So before you press 'Send', reread what you've written and put yourself in the shoes of the person who'll be reading it. You might just find a better way to get your message across.

Before you press 'Send', reread what you've written…

69

Put it into action

Speak or write?

It is so easy and quick to type an email or message to someone. You can type a message more quickly than making a telephone call or going to see someone face to face. The secret is to aim to avoid regretting what, how and with whom you communicated.

This is easily achieved by investing a time upfront thinking about the following:

- What is the intention of the communication?
- What outcome do you need to achieve (e.g. just to let someone know the facts, to seek a response or to have a detailed discussion)?
- Who exactly needs to receive the communication? Who needs to be cc'ed or bcc'ed in the email?
- Does the communication need a more human touch – face to face or by phone? Or is it time to send a handwritten letter?
- Most importantly – will you regret sending the email or SMS?

Save a draft

There are times when you will write an email or SMS that has the potential to make the recipient angry, upset or sad. To avoid regretting what you send, get into the habit of writing your email or SMS and saving it as a draft. Then put your phone down or step away from your computer. Come back to your message after a few hours, reread what you have drafted and decide if the wording and tone work. Think about how you would feel if you received the message.

Only press the 'Send' button when you are comfortable.

MAKE FRIENDS WITH FEAR

'I must not fear. Fear is the mind-killer. Fear is the little-death that brings total obliteration.
I will face my fear. I will permit it to pass over me and through me.'

Frank Herbert

Having a phobia of spiders is one thing, but it is the larger fears we carry around with us that can sabotage our chances of having a great life. Fear can be debilitating. It can stop you taking risks for fear of failing, or taking the lead for fear of being ridiculed.

Knowing where your fears come from can help you understand them and explore ways of overcoming their effects. There is a strong link with our parents and how we were brought up. A good friend is afraid to try out new things that appear dangerous because when she was young her mother obsessed over the possibility of her daughter getting injured. Even just the thought of riding a bicycle or ice-skating is enough to put her into a panic now.

But if I had to name the one fear that causes people not to achieve their goals it would be the fear of being successful. In the words of the teacher and author Marianne Williamson 'our deepest fear is not that we are inadequate. Our deepest fear is that we are powerful beyond measure. It is our light, not our darkness, that most frightens us. We ask ourselves, who am I to be brilliant, gorgeous, talented, fabulous?'

Knowing where your fears come from can help you understand them...

70

Put it into action

Face your fears

Don't assume that you can simply ignore your fears by pretending they don't exist. Instead, talk, joke and laugh about them. Bring them out into the open and in doing so, little by little, you will learn to live with them, making it easier to act in spite of them. In the words of an ancient Japanese proverb, fear is only as deep as the mind allows. It is all in your mind and you can change the part that fears play in your life.

Start by seeking out your fears. It sounds counter-intuitive, but do what you fear, be what you fear and say what you fear. Many studies have confirmed that exposing yourself to your fears is a very effective way of overcoming them.

Today do the thing you fear most. Going up to a high viewing platform can help you overcome vertigo, making public speeches can help you become confident in the spotlight, using a lift can help you overcome claustrophobia.

By doing this over time your fears become smaller and smaller.

You may need professional help

Of course, some fears arise from more deep-rooted paranoias and traumas linked to childhood experiences. In these cases, you might benefit from seeing a hypnotherapist or psychologist. Cognitive Behavioural Therapy (CBT) is a common treatment in this instance. It breaks down your problem into smaller parts to help free you from your fears.

TELL THE TRUTH

'We learned about honesty and integrity – that the truth matters... that you don't take shortcuts or play by your own set of rules... and success doesn't count unless you earn it fair and square.'

Michelle Obama

In 2002 MIT's Robert Feldman showed that on average in the space of just a 10-minute conversation we tell two or three lies. Studies give varying results but all show that humans basically lie a lot.

Clearly, there are different sorts of lie, some small and insignificant and some enormous and outrageous. But a lie is still a lie, even if we justify it as a well-intentioned 'white' lie.

Sometimes it seems as if we are becoming desensitized to other people's lack of integrity. Every week the media is full of stories of well-known personalities who have lied or cheated in some way. It's enough to make you wonder if lying and cheating might actually be a shortcut to success. This could take many forms:

- You could lie about your qualifications and work experience on your CV.
- You could pass off other people's ideas and work as your own.
- You could pretend that you love someone to marry into wealth.
- You could create fake salary paperwork when applying for a bank loan.

A lot of people are happy to live with lies like this, saying they're only small or a smart way to cheat the system. Do or say whatever you want but, if you go down this track, your success will be fake. Your wins will be meaningless. Success without integrity is like building a house without foundations. At some point it will crack and the building will subside.

Success without integrity is like building a house without foundations.

71

Put it into action

Stop fooling yourself

It is time to live with full integrity. From today, make yourself feel bad about lying and cheating. Allow your conscience to rise up and make you feel uncomfortable. Always speak the truth and, if you choose not to, be clear why.

Always be honest with yourself. No more standing in the mirror and lying to the person staring back at you. The Brazilian novelist Paulo Coelho put it so well when he said, 'If you want to be successful, you must respect one rule – never lie to yourself.'

Every action has a consequence

If you do lie and cheat, just be ready for the consequences because you will eventually be caught out. Your house of cards might look fantastic but can collapse in a split second. Your reputation, employment prospects or even freedom could be destroyed. No one looks at Lance Armstrong today and sees a seven-time Tour de France winner.

The thing about lying is that you can never know with certainty the risk of being discovered or the severity of the consequences. You could work your entire career pretending you have a university degree or you might be found out during your first job.

Be ready to answer the question – can you live with the consequences of being found out? And by the way the answer should always be 'No, I cannot!'

BECOME AN EXPERT AT SOMETHING

'Never become so much of an expert that you stop gaining expertise. View life as a continuous learning experience.'

Denis Waitley

You are an expert. In fact, we are all experts in something, even if it is only bad habits that we repeat and practise so often that we master them. Success comes from no longer doing those things that you don't want to be an expert in – like showing off, not listening to others or being lazy – and making room in your life for things you do want to be an expert in. It is about refocusing your internal energy and motivation on what could be called the optimal areas of mastery – those areas in which you would be proud of being called an expert, such as:

- soft skills and behaviours such as being empathic or collaborative
- life skills such as personal financial planning or being a parent
- work skills such as being able to use a computer system or able to manage projects
- professional expertise in a field such as engineering, nursing or law.

You can work to be expert in just one area or develop skills and expertise across several. I moved from finance to recruiting to coaching, during which time I mastered key skills such as thinking strategically, optimally running businesses and leading people. All of this expertise now comes together in my work in the leadership coaching field.

Success comes from no longer doing those things that you don't want to be an expert in and making room in your life for things you do want to be an expert in.

72

Put it into action

Expert at what?

What do you want to be an expert at? Think about why and how such mastery will help you be more successful in your life. As you gain experience, you will have a better idea of what you want to be expert in. If in doubt, simply try to excel and master everything that comes your way. It might seem like common sense but it is easier to become expert in activities that you love doing where you bring passion and energy to your tasks.

Deliberate practice

Expertise takes time and practice. In the words of W. Clement Stone: 'Try, try, try, and keep on trying is the rule that must be followed to become an expert in anything.' Much has been written about the need to practise for 10,000 hours to become an expert. Recent studies have debunked this, but no matter how long it takes you cannot master something overnight. You need to deliberately repeat an activity and seek feedback and mentoring. And, most importantly, you need to make and learn from failures and mistakes. I like to think that the expert is the one who has made the most mistakes.

Pass on your expertise

Teach what you need to master. You might wonder how you can share what you haven't yet mastered but expertise is a relative term and you can always get better at anything that you do. Sharing your insights, experience and knowledge can help you assimilate and understand them better – no matter whether it is renovating a house or completing a tax return.

APOLOGIZE WHEN YOU ARE WRONG

'A man must be big enough to admit his mistakes, smart enough to profit from them, and strong enough to correct them.'

John C. Maxwell

It is a sign of maturity and wisdom when someone freely puts their hands up, admits they made a mistake and apologizes. So many people refuse to acknowledge when they are wrong, preferring to blame others and avoiding taking personal responsibility.

Why is apologizing so hard to do? What are you afraid of? Making an apology isn't weak and soft; in fact, it's quite the opposite. Living a life avoiding apologizing for mistakes that might have hurt other people shows a lack of empathy combined with stubbornness.

When I spend time with people who have a problem with apologizing I often discover that in their hearts they know they have done wrong and that they ought to apologize but somehow their pride and ego hold them back from being contrite and humbly saying 'I am sorry for what I have done.' Apologizing and seeking forgiveness are liberating. It removes guilt and hurt from relationships.

Apologizing and seeking forgiveness are liberating.

73

Put it into action

Authentic apologies, please

The ultimate sign of wisdom, character and integrity is to:

- always tell someone you are sorry
- be open and, if necessary, make a public apology
- make sure that the apology is genuine and said with true intention
- offer to right the wrong.

Words are not enough

Admitting you are wrong and then apologizing is not enough. You might have cleared the air by being open, ensured that others are not incorrectly being blamed or accused, and made the affected parties feel better. However, it is only through your actions that you can truly demonstrate that your apology was genuinely made. You should do two things:

- Make up for what you have done wrong. You might redo what was broken, give some form of compensation, make a more public apology to the group of friends or colleagues involved and/or give an apology card or a gift to the person you have upset.
- Change your behaviour so that when a similar situation arises again you will not repeat your actions. It might be that you make extra effort to remember a birthday, be on time for a meeting or be civil to your sister at the next family gathering.

STAY IN TOUCH WITH OLD FRIENDS

'One of the most beautiful qualities of true friendship is to understand and to be understood.'

Lucius Seneca

There's a Native American saying, 'Don't allow the grass to grow on the path of friendship.' Do everything you can to keep your friendships alive. Friendships that survive the years are a great foundation for a life. It's wonderful to have people you can link up with whenever you want for whatever reasons. They don't all have to be close friends; acquaintances are important, too. By keeping in some form of contact you will be surprised how any type of friendship deepens over time. Friends help connect you with who you are – with your past memories and experiences and the things you have shared with them from your most beautiful dreams through to your darkest secrets.

Friends can serve as a grounding influence. They may have known you when you were just starting out and seen your struggles, failures and successes. That puts them in a privileged position to be your most important mentors, counsellors and advisors. A shared history builds trust and, when trust exists, it is easier to open up and reveal your fears, worries and concerns.

Do everything you can to keep your friendships alive.

74

Put it into action

Whom could you reconnect with?

Think about the friends you have lost touch with. Thanks to technology, it's probably easy to find them, if you want to. A quick search on Google, Wikipedia, Facebook or LinkedIn will often point you to anybody you might want to reconnect with from your past.

Find out if the friendship is still alive

Take a lead in reaching out to them. Discover if they remember you and if they value your friendship and want to rekindle it. Be ready to accept if they're happy to move on and lose touch. It's hard not to take this personally but try not to let it affect you. It might be the case that you are simply too much of a reminder of a past they are trying to move on from. Perhaps they are now married and connecting with you only serves to remind him or her of their carefree and single past, a time they are now happy to let go of/move on from.

KEEP THE BIGGER PICTURE IN MIND

'Try to maintain the perspective that, in time, everything disintegrates and returns to its
initial form.'

Richard Carlson

Small things in life can be upsetting. Whether it's the size of your salary increase or someone stealing your parking space – they may be small but they can still get under your skin.

As the author Dennis Sharpe said, 'Why do you dwell on things that don't matter when
there are so many things that do?' Part of the answer lies in what is actually influencing you
at any moment. So often the bigger picture is not visible and gets temporarily overlooked.
We become transfixed by a small event and fail to step back and look around. It is as if we
are in a theatre and can see only part of the play or show.

When I coach people who seem to be getting caught up in 'sweating the small stuff', I often
ask them to explore the question 'Will this matter tomorrow, next week or in a year's time?'
Thinking about the issues right in front of you like this can help you regain your perspective.

Ask yourself: 'Will this matter tomorrow, next week or in a year's time?'

75

Put it into action

Go up to the balcony

Imagine you are in the theatre standing in front of the stage. You can see and hear all the tiniest mistakes made by the cast and orchestra. It's annoying and distracting. Now go up to the highest balcony and continue watching. Your balcony view provides a new perspective, enabling you to see the show in all its glory without the small irritations that were distracting you before. It's the same show, but taking a step back has transformed your experience of it.

This is what you need to do with the small stuff in your life, too. Ask yourself: 'In the bigger scheme of things, is the event that upsets me really worth my time and attention? Is my team member's imperfect piece of work really so bad? Is the meeting starting late such a problem?'

Does it really matter at the end the day?

If you still struggle to keep things in perspective and find yourself becoming stressed and angry over a multitude of things, try to remember that life is short. On your deathbed you won't care that John beat you to a job promotion or that your neighbour's newly painted house makes yours look rundown.

Protect yourself from unnecessary stress, anxiety and negative emotions by:

- ignoring things that would normally have annoyed you
- letting other people win arguments
- closing your eyes, counting to ten and thinking calm thoughts
- laughing at yourself for taking things too seriously
- encouraging others to take a step back on to their own balcony.

EMBRACE TECHNOLOGY

'Technology is the campfire around which we tell our stories.'
Laurie Anderson

The world around us is increasingly based on technology. Things that were science fiction just a few years ago are now mainstream, like Internet-enabled home appliances and video calls. Mastering technology will certainly help you live a richer and more meaningful life whether that's running a business from your laptop or controlling your home's heating system via your smartphone. The choices and opportunities afforded by technology are growing exponentially each year.

Sure, technology does have its downsides. As Carrie Snow writes: 'Technology ... is a queer thing. It brings you great gifts with one hand, and it stabs you in the back with the other.' Technology can frustrate as much as it can liberate. You're not alone if you've ever bemoaned the limited battery life of a smartphone, had to re-enter a long list of personal data into a misfiring web form or been the victim of cybercrime, malware or viruses. But embracing the positive benefits of technology will increase your efficiency, keep you connected, keep you informed and keep you successful.

Embracing the positive benefits of technology will ... keep you successful.

76

Put it into action

Embrace the future with a positive mindset

- Recognize that you have no choice but to embrace technology. As everything from bank-ing to shopping moves online, it's really no longer optional.

- Don't feel you have to be an early adopter of every gadget, app and new technology that comes along.

- Understand and observe what is available and what each gadget or service can offer you.

- Take an interest in what's new, keep an eye on the tech that kids are excited about and have a go with your friend's new smartphone. Be open-minded in trying to understand what is available and what benefits new technologies bring.

- Make a personal choice about which new gadgets and solutions you choose to adopt. Do not follow the sheep and buy a smartwatch just because everybody else in your local gym is wearing one.

- Use the Internet wisely taking care to protect yourself from all forms of cybercrime. Such crime might include everything from people stealing your online banking details to steal-ing your identity and posing as you on social-media sites.

- Use passwords that are not easy to guess on your devices and on websites that require one.

PERSIST AND DON'T GIVE UP

'Our greatest weakness lies in giving up. The most certain way to succeed is always to try just one more time.'

Thomas A. Edison

If you are happy to be an average student, employee, partner, boss, athlete or friend, then simply do as much as most people do. Skim-read books, don't bother rehearsing your PowerPoint presentation and do the minimum you need to do to get by. The majority of people give up difficult things too easily and stop trying after a first rejection, practice session, failure or disappointment.

It is far too easy to give up and make lame excuses – 'I would have found a job but I am too over-qualified', 'I would have kept training for the charity run, but I am too busy'.

When trying to achieve anything in your life – especially something that in your heart you badly want – never stop and never give up too soon. You don't know how close you might be to the winning line. Instead, persist; be the person who has that one extra attempt, who continues whatever it is that others have stopped doing. Sheer persistence will always get you there in the end.

...never stop and never give up too soon.

77

Put it into action

Know when the 'giving in' moment is appearing

Learn to spot when you are reaching that 'on the verge of quitting' moment. In that moment you will need to 'overcome' something to enable you to continue, to persist in whatever it is you are trying to achieve. Knowing when the moment's coming means you can be ready for it.

In order to persist, you may have to overcome feelings of disappointment, physical or emotional pain, the overwhelming desire to duck out and relax, an urgent need to be like everyone else who has already given up, or a sudden belief that it is impossible to succeed.

In this moment seek out friends, colleagues or family who do not want you to give up, who will remind you about the importance of your dreams and goals.

Be thick-skinned

Dig deep and be ready to ignore voices – both in your head and coming from unsupportive people, telling you:

- 'It's OK, you have done enough.'
- 'No need to go any further.'
- 'You can always try another day.'
- 'No need to stand out and show us up.'
- 'Stop it, you are successful enough.'
- 'Why are you bothering to try so hard?'
- 'You will never succeed so why bother?'

As painful as it might sound, recognize that many people are jealous of what you might achieve – jealous that someone is willing to persist and potentially outshine or outperform them. Never stop trying to achieve a dream on the basis of someone else's advice.

WATCH OUT FOR ADDICTIONS

'Anything that you can become obsessed with, and you do so much that you don't do the things you need to do with family, friends, school, job - that can be an addiction. And texting absolutely can qualify.'

Dale Archer

We are all liable to be afflicted with one addiction or another during our lives. Some can seem harmless but others can literally kill you. Carl Jung claimed that every form of addiction is bad, no matter whether it's alcohol, morphine or idealism. I don't know if this is true but I know that it's how you work and live with them that matters.

The traditional addictions of smoking and drinking might be declining but technology and Internet addictions seem to be taking their place. You might have personally experienced or observed in others a vast array of potentially addictive or obsessive behaviours:

- the workaholic who never seems to leave work to go home
- the shopaholic who never has any money left at the month's end
- the teenager who spends all waking hours playing Internet games
- the intelligent person who always needs to show that he is the brightest in the room.

What are your addictions? Does addictive or compulsive behaviour affect your ability to be successful? Even if the answer is 'no', take time to think about any habits you have that may have crossed the border into obsession or addiction.

Does addictive or compulsive behaviour affect your ability to be successful?

78

Put it into action

Admit it

Be honest with yourself about what patterns of behaviour you have and what you are compulsively or obsessively doing. Take the time today to do a personal audit of your habits and behaviours.

When you have a complete list, annotate each behaviour with observations on how the behaviour impacts upon your life and affects:

- how others view you
- your ability to work well
- your relationships with other people
- your health
- your ability to achieve your future plans and goals.

It's now crunch decision time: how important is it to you to overcome your addictive or compulsive behaviour? Are the negative effects causing you sufficient pain to force you to act?

Sometimes moderation is enough

With some behaviours and actions it might be enough for you to tone down and reduce the frequency, for example getting over your need to win every discussion, cutting down your drinking at the weekend or no longer crying every time someone upsets you.

Seek help

With addictions where you find it impossible to control your impulses and actions, you cannot recover on your own. These addictions can have deep psychological causes and require some form of therapy. Thankfully, today there are many therapy and support groups for all kinds of addictions – gambling, sex, shopping, narcotics, alcohol, spouse abuse, and so on. Many are modelled on the Alcoholics Anonymous groups with their 12-step recovery programme. Deep inner exploration and honesty are part of the process.

SPEND MORE TIME OUTSIDE IN NATURE

'Look deep into nature, and then you will understand everything better.'
Albert Einstein

A 2009 study in the *Journal of Epidemiology and Community Health* showed that you are less likely to be stressed or be anxious when you live or work near greenery. The Japanese call it 'forest bathing'. By simply walking through woods and forests you lower your blood pressure and stress levels. Spending time outside brings so many benefits:

- Natural sunlight gives you much-needed vitamin D, a healthy skin tone and has a positive impact on your demeanour. Your lungs will benefit from the fresh air and this in turn boosts your immune system.
- Getting away from buildings and technology makes you happier, more at peace and more grounded. Working or talking beside a tree that might have been standing for hundreds of years or beside a river can be very cathartic.

Spending time outside opens your mind and sharpens your thinking. I often coach clients while walking in a park or beside water rather than just sitting in a meeting room or restaurant together. It enables a more open and reflective conversation and insights to emerge.

Nature reminds you to be calm, patient and to give things time. All around you in nature plants grow surely and slowly as the seasons pass. In the words of the American author and naturalist Hal Borland: 'Knowing trees, I understand the meaning of patience. Knowing grass, I can appreciate persistence.'

Spending time outside opens your mind and sharpens your thinking.

79

Put it into action

Be outside in nature as often as your life will allow. There are many ways to do this and here are three of my own favourites:

Take up gardening

Being in nature doesn't need to involve a long drive; it can be just as good to go to your local park or work on your balcony overlooking trees.

A wonderful way to be in nature, though, is to actually look after a garden. It might be yours, a friend's or simply some potted plants on your window ledge. There is nothing more invigorating, energizing and healing than to spend a few hours a week pottering around watering, weeding, making compost, pruning and feeding passing birds.

Getting your hands dirty and feeling the earth is one of the best ways of de-stressing, of stepping away from your daily struggles and being in the moment.

Spend your holidays with nature

I have a cousin who loves spending all of her holidays in remote places – the Isle of Skye, the Falkland Islands, the Arizona desert. She loves to watch birds and to spend hours sitting with nature all around her. Why not emulate her and shy away from noisy holidays in large hotel complexes or modern cities? Vacations in the countryside can be the best way of recovering – from physical illness, emotional upset, stress or unhappiness.

See the stars

Hunt out a place away from light pollution where you can see the universe in all its glory with the Milky Way streaking across the night sky. A telescope will help but is not essential. The experience is sure to fill you with awe, and remind you that your troubles and concerns are small as they pale into insignificance in the bigger picture before your eyes. There is no better way to put your life's troubles and concerns into perspective than watching the skies.

USE YOUR INTELLIGENCE WISELY

'Everybody is a genius. But if you judge a fish by its ability to climb a tree, it will spend its
whole life thinking it's stupid.'

Albert Einstein

When it comes to brainpower, it's easy to be strong in one area but not in another. You
might be fantastic at crosswords but find it impossible to get your head around the instruc-
tions for using a new household appliance; you might sail through intellectual challenges
at work but struggle to deal with the simultaneous questions and demands of your three
children at home.

According to the Cattell–Horn–Carroll (CHC) theory, our brains possess ten broad abilities
that in turn are broken down into 70 narrow abilities. These vary from how fast you process
information through to the ability to deal with unfamiliar information. You don't have to
master all 70 to be a success and your challenge is not to know how intelligent you are,
but rather to know what kinds of intellectual skill you need to possess in order to achieve
success in different aspects of your life. Do you already have the skills you need and do you
know how to use them, or do you need to acquire them from scratch?

Everything we do requires more intelligence than ever before. You don't need to be the
smartest at everything, but consciously developing intelligence in areas that are going to
help you will pay huge dividends.

…consciously developing intelligence in areas that are going to help you will pay huge
dividends.

80

Put it into action

Develop what you have

The key to your success is to focus on your existing strengths while also developing those areas that will help you achieve your goals in life. Think about your goals and what intellectual strengths would support them most? Establish what you need and focus on that.

You could also try developing areas where you are weak even if you don't think you would ever need these skills. A great memory may not seem particularly important to you but you never know when it could be useful – and you could have fun doing memory exercises.

Making time to maintain a good all-round intelligence works wonders for your morale and self-esteem. It has also been shown to slow down cognitive illnesses such as dementia and Alzheimer's. Find time for challenging pursuits such as completing crosswords, other paper challenges such as Sudoku, and games such as chess and backgammon. Always be willing to learn new things to keep your brain regularly stimulated and challenged.

Never show off

Intelligence alone is not enough and being invited to join Mensa is no guarantee of success in your life. You need to be able to apply your intelligence and use it well around other people. This is where you need to be street smart with a good dose of common sense and to have developed your emotional intelligence skills.

No matter how much more intelligent you appear, or think you are, never make others feel small or less intelligent than you. This is an abuse of your skill, makes you look arrogant, snobbish and condescending, and will turn people against you.

FOCUS ON CHARACTER NOT POPULARITY

'I don't care whether people like me or dislike me. I'm not on earth to win a popularity contest. I'm here to be the best human being I possibly can be.'

Tab Hunter

We live in a 'Like' culture. Facebook, YouTube and Instagram have made it normal for grown-up people to obsess about comments and Likes. Are we really all so desperate to be noticed and loved by everyone around us? To what end exactly? This sort of popularity doesn't last and chasing it simply diverts you from searching for your own happiness, fulfilment and growth. As the American journalist Horace Greeley said, 'Fame is a vapor, popularity an accident, and riches take wing. Only one thing endures and that is character.'

The growth of reality-TV shows looking for the best singer or dancer encourages the idea that popularity is something to aim for in itself. They perpetuate the idea that it is good to be the one with most votes, views or Likes. But is the person with 100,000 Twitter followers really happy and content? This apparent popularity is a real measure of what? All it really shows is that a lot of people showed a passing fancy and clicked the 'Like' button.

In the real world, how long will the prom queen, head girl or sportsperson of the year feel fulfilled, successful and happy just because they won a popularity contest? The actress Mia Wasikowska put it so well when she said: 'Popularity is very inconsistent. Sometimes it's there, sometimes it's not. It usually just comes in waves.'

'Only one thing endures and that is character.'

81

Put it into action

Be popular with yourself

The only person whose popularity you need is your own. Learn to value, accept and love yourself.

How you choose to express yourself should be in ways that support you.

Stop defining yourself by what others think and say of you. Instead, look inside yourself and define yourself by what you feel and think.

Learn not to worry if your choices are not popular with other people. The important people in your life will not think less of you or stop liking you simply because you choose to do what you want whether it's covering your back with a weird tattoo, quitting your job to pursue a crazy dream or to stop wearing make-up.

Do the right thing no matter how unpopular

To let yourself do something that may not be popular and could leave you rejected by other people is not easy. We want to be loved and accepted by other people and as a result are very reluctant to let others down. When you choose to 'be in the crowd' and to 'make your family proud' what are you allowing yourself to give up, what part of you are you not expressing? You don't need to go out with colleagues for evening drinks just to be in with the group, you don't need to wear fashionable clothes to help you fit in with others and you don't need to copy other people's music, reading or restaurant choices.

Starting today make choices which are right for you, to help you achieve your life goals and dreams. If you must view life as a popularity contest, then make yourself your only judge.

SAY GOODBYE TO TOXIC PEOPLE

'Toxic relationships not only make us unhappy; they corrupt our attitudes and dispositions in ways that undermine healthier relationships and prevent us from realizing how much better things can be.'

Michael Josephson

In Chapter 38 I spoke about the need to avoid polluting environments, but the biggest danger is being polluted by people around you. They might be your friends, family members or colleagues who fill the air with negativity, scepticism or jealousy, who are always moaning and wanting but never giving. We can all have moments like this but what makes someone toxic is the persistence in how they act with and around you.

You will almost certainly have experienced several of these scenarios:

- the colleague who insists on always being right
- the parent who constantly puts you down, tramples on your dreams and ambitions and tells you what you are not capable of achieving in your life
- the friend who is always dishonest with you
- the person who always wants something from you – your time, money and energy – but finds excuses for not helping when you are in need
- the friend who is always trying to dictate what you should do and think
- the person who has a knack of pressuring you into doing things you do not want to do.

I coach so many individuals whose struggles seem to stem solely from being connected to incredibly negative, nasty or bitter people. Isn't it time that you bid such people goodbye?

...the biggest danger is being polluted by people around you.

82

Put it into action

Wake-up time

It's tempting to try to always see the good in people and to rationalize bad behaviour but it's time to wake up to reality. Rather than trying to excuse people, focus on what is best for you, for your sanity, health and peace of mind.

Only you can judge how toxic their behaviours need to be for you to decide to move away from them – to stop your life becoming suffocated and poisoned by being in their presence. Only you can decide when to walk away but here's a suggestion. Now might be a good time.

Politely reply 'no'

Don't feel guilty or feel the need to justify your decision when you turn down invitations to socialize with a toxic friend or when you avoid a family gathering. The toxic person you're avoiding will never accept that they are a bad influence on you. Better to politely say you have accepted another invitation rather than confront them with it.

Minimize contact

There will be some people you cannot totally walk away from but you can limit your exposure to their influence and energy. Avoid inviting them to your own home and when you do meet them try to keep your time together short. Visit a toxic relative just for the day rather than staying overnight.

LEARN FROM YOUR GRANDPARENTS (BEFORE IT IS TOO LATE)

'We should all have one person who knows how to bless us despite the evidence,.
Grandmother was that person to me.'

Phyllis Theroux

If you're lucky, you'll have grandparents you can spend time with and who care for you, love and guide you. Grandparents can bring you wisdom, understanding and acceptance in ways that are more relevant to your life than you might imagine. You have their DNA and share many aspects of their personality, intelligence and ambitions. They also understand your parents pretty well and can help you navigate those challenges much more easily.

You can't fool your grandparents in the same way that you can your friends, siblings or parents. Perhaps it's their years of experience and accumulated wisdom that means they can see through your justifications, excuses and arguments.

No matter how old you are, your grandparents can bring you so much that others can't because of the deep trust that generally exists between you and them. This will help you open up, share and explore your ideas, concerns, fears and dreams with them.

Because they have lived through many of life's cycles, they bring a different perspective on relationships, joys and despairs, illnesses and deaths, changes and new starts, failures and successes. And because they are more grounded and less emotional than your younger relatives and friends they can help you make sense of life's opportunities and challenges.

Grandparents can bring you wisdom, understanding and acceptance…

83

Put it into action

Spend time with them

If possible, make an extra effort to spend time with your grandparents. Make sure you have enough time to relax and be yourself – sharing your life's ups and downs with them while listening to their thoughts and recollections.

Consider taking a trip with one or more of your grandparents. I once drove with my maternal grandmother from Yorkshire to Wales – just the two of us visiting places where she had lived, meeting her former neighbours and visiting my mother's school. It was grounding and eye-opening. Things like this can help you to understand where you have come from and what your parents and their parents have experienced in their lives.

Not only with grandparents

Your grandparents may no longer be alive or may be too old or infirm to spend time with. What about other older family friends or relatives you've known over the years? I recently reconnected with some of my paternal grandfather's few surviving siblings. Spending time with them has been a wonderful experience allowing me to better understand my past. Whom could you connect with?

Collect their stories

It can be very rich and rewarding to ask relatives to share with you some of their most treasured life stories. Their recollections can give you a very emotional and meaningful connection with your family's past. You might consider recording their words on paper or on camera. Doing this is an opportunity for you to step away from today's busyness and stress and to simply enjoy listening to other people's experiences.

HAVE A TRUE CHARACTER THAT MAKES YOU PROUD

> 'Be more concerned with your character than your reputation, because your character is what you really are, while your reputation is merely what others think you are.'
>
> John Wooden

What are you like when no one is watching? It is said that you can judge a person's true character by what they do when no one is around. In these moments are you generous, lazy, mean, thoughtful, honest or hard-working? Are you the same person as when you are in company? How would you describe your character – that combination of your behaviours, values, styles and mindset?

Through my work I have come to conclude that our true characters can be our Achilles' heel – the thing that trips us up on our road to genuine success. So many people go through life hiding parts of their character from view.

Do not be surprised when in moments of anger or stress you see someone's true personality reveal itself, destroying the carefully crafted image they've been portraying up until that moment. Cultivate a character that you can be proud of so that the private you is the same you that you show the world.

What are you like when no one is watching?

84

Put it into action

Commit to iron out your character flaws

The only way to live a life of genuine success is to work on your character, particularly those areas that you may prefer to hide. Overcoming or eliminating flaws in your character is not easy. You may have been carrying them around with you since your childhood and they could be ingrained in who you are.

If you are very clear on the areas you need to focus on, you can get started immediately. If in doubt, try some of these techniques:

- Start observing yourself and keeping notes about what you see. When are you suppressing yourself in order to hide a behaviour? What embarrasses you about yourself? What would you not want a new boss, partner or colleague to observe you being like?
- Seek the opinion of a few close friends or family, exploring with them how authentically you come across and how consistent you are in terms of your character traits.
- Take a personality assessment test such as the Hogan assessment, a questionnaire-based tool that is renowned for revealing a person's dark or shadowy side, especially how you act and appear when stressed or upset.
- Learn from any 360-degree feedback that you might have received in recent years in your place of work.

Help others to explore their own character flaws

There's little point in ironing out your own flaws if you are living and working with people who constantly put their own poor character traits on show. While you're trying to clean up your own act it might be uncomfortable living with other people's weaknesses. Have the courage and diplomatic skills to let others be aware of their flaws but do it sparingly and save it for people you really care about.

PRACTISE GRATITUDE

'Let us be grateful to the people who make us happy; they are the charming gardeners who make our souls blossom.'

Marcel Proust

What do you have to be grateful for today?

Being thankful is good for your health. In a 2015 University of California study those who exhibited higher levels of gratitude were shown to have better-quality sleep, more positive moods and less symptoms of potential heart failure. Earlier studies had pointed to increased optimism and ease of making new friends as a result of having a more thankful disposition.

Unfortunately, it's easier to see faults than find cause for thanks. Losing sight of the big picture in favour of some inconvenient detail has become a default position for many people. If you've ever heard someone fresh out of hospital focusing on the time taken to be treated and the quality of the hospital food rather than on the fact that they are safe and well with their illness cured, you'll understand this all too well.

We've lost that ability to simply be thankful for what we've got. Maybe we're too busy, more caught up in our own lives. The Internet has certainly encouraged us all to build up expectations of what we're entitled to or what our expectations should be. The end result is that we judge and complain rather than being thankful.

If you truly wish to stand out and to be successful, start by simply being grateful and demonstrating sincere thanks.

Be grateful and demonstrate sincere thanks.

85

Put it into action

Allow yourself to show gratitude all the time

This might take a slight mentality shift, but from today try to live each day with a 'glass is full' mindset, always looking to give thanks to others and to feel thankful inside. Try to consciously put gratitude and thanks ahead of criticism. Gracious and empathic people find it effortless to show gratitude to others and to not focus on being critical. If that's hard for you, look around you for inspiration – is there someone who seems to show thanks without any effort or questions asked?

Identify whom you're grateful to

Explore who has earned your gratitude by asking yourself: 'What am I truly grateful for in my life?' List the things you're thankful for and trace them back to the people who've earned your gratitude. The names on your list might be obvious and will probably include parents, partners and other family members, but it might also throw up some surprises.

Be creative in how you demonstrate your gratitude. Follow up your thoughts with words and deeds.

Keep a gratitude journal

Write down each day a couple of things you are grateful for. It doesn't matter how large or inconsequential, just keep a note of them all in a gratitude journal. Alongside each one, note down whom you thanked or will thank and how.

FOCUS ON GOOD NEWS

'Bad news sells because the amygdala is always looking for something to fear.'
Peter Diamandis

The world is full of bad news and how you handle that is critical for your state of mind. For many, the solution is simply to avoid it. There are plenty of people who decide not to read or watch the news in order to avoid all the negativity and fear it creates. On the surface, this does seem like the ideal solution but, apart from cutting you off from what's happening in the world, there are other implications. The positive side to bad news and events is that confronting it can help you develop your compassion and sense of what is right and wrong. You might even resolve to make the world a better place through doing something positive to counter the bad news.

Your big challenge is to avoid letting the negativity get you down, depress you and lower your energy levels. A constant barrage of external negativity can stop you believing that your dreams and goals can be attained and that you deserve to achieve them. Never allow bad news be an excuse to stop seeking success in life and to feel deserving of a great life.

Never allow bad news be an excuse to stop seeking success in life…

86

Put it into action

Help yourself to stay positive

Tilt your balance towards positive news: for every piece of bad news that you consume try to find at least one piece of good news to counterbalance it. There are many websites focused on sharing positive news (http://www.goodnewsnetwork.org and http://www.huffingtonpost.com/good-news) that can be fun to read. Don't be an ostrich and stick your head in the sand but give yourself daily evidence that there are good things happening in the world too. Do know about world events, and do know about what is happening in your town, but don't dwell on the negative stories to the point that you become fearful, upset, cynical and unable to positively focus on what you are doing.

Change the conversation

It's easy for conversations to become stuck on upsetting or depressing topics, particularly when they're looming large in the news. Don't be afraid to be the one to move things on, saying: 'Isn't that enough depressing discussion about...? What about discussing...?' or 'I think we have analysed this topic to death. What other interesting things have been happening?'

It will probably come as a relief to those around you that someone has had the courage to change the topic. In spite of what newspaper publishers and TV news editors think, most people do not enjoy focusing on negative or bad news.

GENUINE SUCCESS CANNOT BE FAKED

'We are what we pretend to be, so we must be careful about what we pretend to be.'
Kurt Vonnegut

All of us are pretending to a greater or lesser extent. We pretend we're happy, in control, in love, financially fine or simply that all is well. It's hard to know what's real and what's make-believe at times with everyone projecting such a wonderful image of themselves. You see this in social-media posts, in people living beyond their means and racking up credit-card debts and in our conversations where we say we're well and everything's fine. I am constantly surprised at what's actually going on behind my clients' masks, how happy they are to act successful when in reality the opposite is true.

I have seen people spend years giving the impression of material success when behind the facade they are on the verge of bankruptcy and faced with enormous personal debts. I have worked with a newly promoted rising star who always appeared gung-ho, positive and ambitious before revealing how he hates his career, long hours and the pretence of liking the expectations that go with his salary.

The truth is, it's easy to fool other people – with a smile, a nice suit, cool holidays, speaking highly of what you have – but you can't fool yourself. Genuine success means fulfilling your dreams, passions and life goals. *Pretending* that you are doing that when you are not is living a lie. Your true feelings, needs and ambitions will reveal themselves at some point however deeply you bury them – and it won't look pretty. Be careful.

Your true feelings, needs and ambitions will reveal themselves at some point however deeply you bury them…

87

Put it into action

Be honest

In the words of poet and photographer Tyler Knott Gregson be someone who can confidently say 'I would rather wear honest tears than the most beautiful and elaborately faked smile.' Your challenge is to let go of the modern notion that you can have everything and be anything you ever dreamed of. Step away from a life of multiple overused credit cards, fake CVs and diplomas and pretending to others about how well you are doing.

Accept that life is a journey and that your road to success on any front takes time. Allow yourself to step away from pretending to your family, friends and colleagues that you are successful when you know that you still have a long way to go.

You can fake something

There is one area of your life where it's OK to pretend and that's with your attitude and mindset. Pretending when you want to change your behaviours is OK. Practising what you want to become, or faking it until you make it, is a positive and successful way to help you change some aspect of your personality and attitude.

GROW OLD DISGRACEFULLY

'At age 20, we worry about what others think of us. At age 40, we don't care what they think of us. At age 60, we discover they haven't been thinking of us at all.'

Ann Landers

You are never too old to chase another goal, dream a new dream or crazily act out your desires. How else can you claim to have lived a successful life if you can't use your freedom to be yourself?

The beautiful thing about getting old is the moment you realize that there really isn't anyone out there whose expectations and norms you still need to meet. Once you've discovered that, you'll never say 'I am too old to do that' again. Getting older reduces your need to conform and impress people. When you're younger you might have children to bring up, a job to keep and a mortgage to pay off. As those responsibilities fade into the background, it frees you up to express the real you.

It's wonderful to question what is stopping you doing and being who you really want to be and it can be liberating to anticipate a time when you won't be held back by others' expectations. Knowing this can help you enjoy some of that freedom even earlier in life. Life is too short to live other people's neatly manicured view of what you should be like. While you still have the energy, health and wealth is the time to truly live your life. If not now, then when?

You are never too old to chase another goal.

88

Put it into action

Stop holding back

What hobbies, passions and desires have you let yourself leave on the top shelf as you focused on having a career, family and home? Take them down and clean off the dust and cobwebs. Allow yourself to reconnect with those fantastic and crazy aspects of your self. It might be that childlike curiosity, joy of singing, love of dancing or a passion for trying out new things. Who cares how old you are?

Be honest and open

You do not have to justify your choices. It doesn't matter if people laugh at your choice of beachwear or your love of rave music. You don't have to seek permission or support for your choices. Your family and friends may think you have gone mad. Be honest and tell them that you are fulfilling your dreams and desires. Do not allow anyone to make you feel ashamed or guilty. Be proud of yourself.

BREATHE WELL

'For breath is life, and if you breathe well you will live long on earth.'
Sanskrit proverb

When was the last time you thought about your breathing? You probably cannot remember, but it's the most important thing you do in your life – in fact, you wouldn't be here for long without it. You breathe in different ways depending on what you are thinking, doing or experiencing. When you are stressed, anxious, afraid or worried, your breaths become fast, shallow and noisy. On the other hand, when you are relaxed, you may have no sense of breathing at all, your lungs work so slowly and silently.

Just as circumstances can affect how you breathe, so your breathing also influences and changes you. It is no coincidence that we say to somebody who is feeling panicked to 'take a deep breath'. Breathing optimally can improve your physical and mental wellbeing in so many ways. There have been numerous studies of the benefits of optimal breathing which have concluded that really good deep breathing has these positive benefits:

- It releases tension and makes you feel better and happier through the release of neuro-chemicals.
- It makes your heart stronger, strengthens your immune system, helps remove toxins and makes you more energetic through higher levels of oxygen flowing through your body.
- It improves many of your body functions and organs including your nervous system, quality of your blood, digestion and your lungs.

Who would have thought that focusing your attention on something as natural as breathing could have such profound benefits?

Your breathing influences and changes you.

89

Put it into action

Practise deep breathing

Start observing how you breathe and how it changes during the day. Are you breathing through your mouth, nose or a combination of both? Do you see changes in the speed of breathing depending on how you feel and what you are doing? How often do you take a deep breath?

Even when totally relaxed and calm your body may not breathe very deeply, particularly if you are in the habit of taking shallow breaths. This type of breathing is a common symptom of today's fast-paced world of stress, busyness and non-stop activities. Deep breaths are the best way to breathe but it takes concentration and practice. Interestingly, as far back as ancient Greece, doctors advised their patients to practise deep breathing.

Here's how to do it:

- Breathe slowly and calmly using your nose to inhale and your mouth to exhale.
- Breathe in slowly for up to 5 seconds, imagining that as you inhale air you are filling your stomach, not just your lungs.
- Hold your breath for 3–4 seconds before exhaling.

Whenever you are conscious of your breathing, repeat this pattern. Over time you should find that you start breathing like this even when you are not consciously aware of doing so.

Find clean air

It goes without saying that, no matter how well you breathe, you will harm yourself if the air you inhale is dirty and unhealthy. If you live or work in polluted air, seriously consider relocating. In the words of Edward Abbey, aim to 'breathe deep of that yet sweet and lucid air', rather than air that is stale or full of harmful particles and gases.

TRAVEL FAR

'Perhaps travel cannot prevent bigotry, but by demonstrating that all peoples cry, laugh, eat, worry, and die, it can introduce the idea that if we try and understand each other, we may even become friends.'

Maya Angelou

My grandfather used to encourage me to travel the world by saying 'Travel is the only thing you can buy that actually makes you richer.' Leaving the comfort of your familiar surroundings can be the most eye-opening experience of your life. There's something about the magical combination of freedom from the everyday and exposure to the new and unexpected.

Getting away can be the best way of opening your heart and mind. A few days or weeks in a foreign city can show you how other people live, see the world and tackle the issues in their lives. It's an opportunity to become more compassionate, understanding and perhaps less narrow-minded. Simply trekking through a poorer part of the world will remind you how fortunate and lucky you are or visiting the Middle East will give you a new perspective on the conflicts there and the refugee crisis.

There is a lovely Moorish proverb that says that 'He who does not travel does not know the value of men.' This is so true. You may not have the finances to travel to distant parts of the globe – only a few of us can afford the time and cost incurred to jet off to distant continents – but travel wherever and whenever you can and you will be richer for it.

...travel wherever and whenever you can and you will be richer for it.

90

Put it into action

Travel as much as you can

Take as much leave as you can and definitely never come to the end of the year with unused holiday allowance.

Use vacations to feed your childlike imagination and sense of awe. Go to new places no matter whether it's an hour's drive or ten hours' flight from your home.

If you are torn between spending your money on things and on holidays, choose holidays.

Brainstorm where you would like to go. Open an atlas and explore. Follow your interests and curiosities. If you want to know more about global warming, go and visit Greenland's glaciers or some of the low-lying islands in the Maldives.

Appreciate and learn from other cultures

Travel with the aim of connecting with the local people, food and culture. Travel with an aim of experiencing new and unexpected things. Get to know new cultures, ways of thinking, cooking and living. When you travel in poorer countries, be with people less fortunate than you and learn how they live their lives.

KEEP A JOURNAL

'My journal is a storehouse, a treasury for everything in my daily life: the stories I hear, the people I meet, the quotations I like, and even the subtle signs and symbols I encounter that speak to me indirectly.'

Dorothy Seyler

Recording your daily thoughts and experiences could be good for your health. There is growing evidence to suggest that keeping a journal contributes to strengthening your immune cells but, regardless of other health benefits, maintaining a daily or weekly diary, journal or blog is a really healthy way of enabling you to:

- record what you have been doing and saying and make sense of it all to see what is most important
- reflect upon your changing thoughts, dreams, hopes, fears, experiences, feelings and opinions
- create solutions for the decisions and choices facing you
- plan ahead with more clarity and thoughtfulness
- develop a thoughtful and reflective relationship with your mind so that you can know yourself better – your blind spots, dreams, goals, fears and challenges.

Whether you choose to be open with your journal or private is up to you but always keep a part of it for your eyes only. This allows you to be extremely honest, open and revealing, enabling you to explore your innermost feelings, worries and desires without fear of comment or judgement.

Recording your daily thoughts and experiences could be good for your health.

91

Put it into action

Start a journal

It doesn't have to be a huge commitment. Just 15–20 minutes a day is enough to start journalling effectively. And remember, there are no rules – just write your innermost thoughts and try not to censor yourself.

Develop your own style

If you are already keeping a diary, notebook or journal, be open to recording your thoughts, feelings and experiences in new and creative ways:

- Rather than writing in a typical bullet-point or essay style, try drawing mind maps where you connect ideas together using key words and phrases.
- Collect newspaper and magazine articles and pictures which have really had an impact on you and capture how you felt at that moment.
- Collect photos if you prefer instead of words and use your journal to create collages.
- Don't feel the need to follow a conventional diary format. Try keeping a notebook of where you save your thoughts by theme. One part might focus on your work and career reflections, another on your financial goals and another on your relationships.
- Include pages written by friends and family. Ask them to complete a blank piece of paper entitled 'My thoughts for today'.

Use technology
- Keep a blog where you capture photos, favourite quotes and thoughts.
- Make sound or video recordings to capture your life and dreams.
- Use social-media pages to share selected posts with friends or a wider circle of people.

LOSE YOURSELF ... AND FIND YOURSELF AGAIN

'When I feel lost and can't make a decision, I just stop and get quiet. I take a time-out.'

Kim Cattrall

We've all faced moments when we've felt lost. As you move through different stages of your life, it can feel at times as though you no longer know where you're going or what you're doing. It's a scary moment to suddenly feel clueless about where life is taking you. It can hit you at different times and in different ways – adolescence, marriage, starting a new job, mid-life, being fired, getting a divorce, when children leave home, bereavement or retirement.

At these moments it is quite common to feel lost. You may feel that your life is drifting, that you're lacking purpose, or you may just be too overwhelmed by the day-to-day to think straight. Realizing that this is normal and that you're not alone is important. Henry Thoreau wrote that 'not until we are lost do we begin to understand ourselves'. Feeling lost is OK. It is simply your mind needing to stop and gather information in order to decide 'What next?' It is a kind of emergency stop mechanism when life is overloading your ability to cope.

For most people, it's a temporary state before their find their way back to their true self. For others, the issue can be more profound and disorienting and it's important to recognize if you need help and seek it out before your mental health suffers.

Feeling lost is OK.

92

Put it into action

Press pause

The common response when we feel lost is to try to fill the space by doing something. As Dr Rollo May says, 'It is an ironic habit of human beings to run faster when we have lost our way.' We hate not knowing and not doing and often default to filling the gap by quickly choosing answers, finding solutions and taking action – *any* action. In reality, the best course of action is to press the pause button. Pausing stops your brain from throwing dozens of different solutions, scenarios, fears and worries at you. This is an important moment in your life to take a really deep breath. In fact, take as many deep breaths as you need to help you through such a moment.

Ask yourself some searching questions

While your pause button is pressed, ask yourself some important questions:

- 'Why am I feeling the way I am?'
- 'What has really changed that is causing me to feel lost?'
- 'What do I really need to do now?'
- 'What are my options moving forward?'
- 'Which of them would I like to pursue?'

There is not a quick fix. You might spend days or even months exploring these questions and allowing your answers to evolve. When you feel ready, calmly and thoughtfully set yourself some actions and goals. These need not be major life goals, just some sensible actions that send you roughly in the direction you want to head.

PLAN AHEAD

'Expect the best, plan for the worst, and prepare to be surprised.'

Denis Waitley

Do you like detailed plans or spontaneity? With small matters in life you can fail to plan without any serious consequences and only a little inconvenience – forgetting to carry an umbrella on a day it pours – but with larger decisions you need to plan more. In reality, we all do a mix of both but each of us has a natural preference for being planning oriented or action oriented. Success is about achieving a balance. You are looking to walk a path between:

1 seizing opportunities that cross your path and positively moving forward, and

2 considering any possible downsides and making suitable contingency plans.

There is no perfect balance. One day you could be feeling rash and overly optimistic while on another you may be too cautious and risk averse. One thing is certain: it's the combination that brings success. By planning ahead, thinking about your goals and setting priorities, you will be in a better position to act when the moment comes.

It's the combination of planning and spontaneity that brings success.

93

Put it into action

Get into a planning habit

Whatever you do in life, give a moment's thought to what could go wrong and the possible outcomes. When you enter into any agreement, have an idea of your exit plan - what you might do if things don't work out as planned. But remember that some of life's most exciting and memorable moments can't have contingency plans placed around them. You simply have to let yourself take a leap of faith following your intuition, gut, soul or heart.

Plan for the worst

At some point in your life, you'll need to think about what happens when you get ill or die and how to make things as easy as possible for the people you're leaving behind. The solution is simple:

- Help your dependants understand your finances - where the paperwork is kept, how to operate your bank accounts and so on.
- Prepare and share a last will and testament.
- Take out a life insurance policy.
- Have other insurance coverage - for your home, for travel and medical emergencies.

TICK OFF YOUR BUCKET LIST

'One day you will wake up and there won't be any more time to do the things you've always wanted. Do it now.'

Paulo Coelho

What do you want to do before you die? www.bucketlist.net carried out a survey asking people for their top ten and it produced some interesting results, with the overall top ten looking like this:

1 See the Northern Lights

2 Skydive

3 Get a tattoo

4 Swim with dolphins

5 Go on a cruise

6 Get married

7 Run a marathon

8 Go zip lining

9 Ride an elephant

10 Go scuba diving.

What stands out about this list is the importance of experiences over *things*. OK, so some of these are going to cost you money, but the majority of them are eminently achievable. You want to run a marathon? What's stopping you pulling on your trainers tomorrow and starting to train?

Most of us are unselfish and we willingly spend our lives helping other people achieve their wishes and dreams, often at the expense of our own. Your focus might be on your own children and extend to parents, nieces, nephews, friends and helping people in need through charitable work. All these things are important but you have to make time for yourself too so that you can start ticking off whatever unfulfilled dreams you have.

The *Shawshank Redemption* contains a classic line: 'Guess it comes down to a simple choice really. Get busy living, or get busy dying.' Isn't it time that you got busy working through your own bucket list?

Get busy working through your own bucket list.

94

Put it into action

Create your bucket list

It's really not hard. Grab a pen and create your own top ten. What are the top ten things you want to do before you leave the planet?

Why not create a collective bucket list for yourself and your loved ones. It can be fun to bond over shared dreams and goals – and even more fun to actually do them. Roll on your next family vacation!

Share your list more widely

Making your bucket list public gives you an added incentive to have to complete your list. On the www.bucketlist.net website you can share your list as well as exploring what others want to do.

Surprise others

If you have been fortunate in life and you've already completed much of your list, why not set about helping other people realize their bucket-list items? There are a number of charities that help raise money and in-kind contributions to enable terminally ill children achieve their dreams before they die.

HELP SUSTAIN THE PLANET

'When the story of these times gets written, we want it to say that we did all we could, and it was more than anyone could have imagined.'

Bono

There's a growing belief that our planet is reaching a tipping point of irreversible ecological change. Whether or not this extreme scenario is true, you must be aware that things are changing:

- It is estimated that each year globally we dispose of 500 billion to 1 trillion plastic bags most of which will take centuries to decompose.
- The world's rain forests are currently being destroyed at a rate equivalent to the size of 100,000 football fields every day.
- One study suggests that, just within the United States, about 40 per cent of all lakes are too polluted for aquatic life to exist or to swim in.
- The World Wildlife Fund says that species are becoming extinct at a rate between 1,000 and 10,000 times higher than the natural extinction rate.
- Over 1 billion people do not have access to safe drinking water.
- By 2030 it is forecast that the number of cars in the world will double.

This is a time when doing nothing is not an option. The unprecedented global changes we are facing will, if left unchecked, make it impossible for future generations to enjoy the lifestyle we have become accustomed to living.

Can you really feel satisfied with your own success if all around you the environment is suffering?

This is a time when doing nothing is not an option.

95

Put it into action

Live more sustainably

There is a lovely Native American proverb that states that we do not inherit the Earth from our ancestors, we borrow it from our children. Every day you have an impact on the environment around you. What you choose to do or not do makes a difference, no matter how small and insignificant it might appear. What differences are you willing to make in how you live? Why not start here:

- Minimize what you waste. A good place to start is in the kitchen. Buy and consume less to avoid contributing to the millions of tonnes of foodstuffs that we throw away each day. Create compost using your food waste and avoid collecting plastic bags when shopping.
- Every time you buy new things for your home give something away to charity shops.
- Invest time in cleaning up your environment, taking part in beach or park clean-ups, for example.
- Be more green in how you live and travel. Switch to a hybrid car, walk and cycle more and take public transportation when possible. Invest in solar panels for your home and make your home energy-efficient. Start calculating your own carbon footprint.

CONNECT WITH SOMETHING BIGGER THAN YOURSELF

'I don't know what your destiny will be, but one thing I do know: the only ones among you who will be really happy are those who have sought and found how to serve.'

Albert Schweitzer

Connecting to something greater than yourself is good for your mental health and will make you a happier person. The founder of the field of positive psychology, Martin Seligman, identified this as vital to a person's wellbeing. What do you connect with? Do you:

- follow a religion of some kind?
- feel strongly about nature and the Earth?
- work with a charity or community to improve the lives of a particular group of people?
- stand up for and fight for some kind of political cause such as women's rights, ending slavery or saving your local village street from being demolished?
- simply focus on giving your family as much time, love and resources as possible to enable them to thrive?

You may not be an active participant in anything, but in truth we all want to be part of something bigger than ourselves. Keeping yourself to yourself cuts you off from other things and people. When I provide coaching to busy and ambitious leaders I often help them to come to similar conclusions as they come to realize that chasing their own career and material dreams is a small part of how they really want to spend their lives.

> Connecting to something greater than yourself is good for your mental health and will make you a happier person.

96

Put it into action

Not sure where to focus?

To find meaningful uses of your time and effort ask yourself a few questions:

- 'When I look around what am I most passionate about?'
- 'Beyond myself and my immediate family what matters most to me in life?'
- 'If I could change one thing about the world what would it be?'

There are no right or wrong answers. You do not have to do anything in particular. Do not feel guilty if you aren't inspired to change the world or to raise millions for a particular charity. Do whatever is real and authentic to you and what makes you feel happy and fulfilled.

More is good for you

The more you jump into things that are greater than you, the more meaning you will find in life. You might be tempted to push back claiming that you are too busy but ironically it is often the busiest people who find the most time to help and support others. To paraphrase Theodore Roosevelt: simply do what you can, whenever you can.

UNLEARN EVERYTHING

'Before people can begin something new, they have to end what used to be and
unlearn the old way.'

William Bridges

It is estimated that 40 per cent of what you learn in college will be out-dated in a decade's time. A large part of my coaching involves helping clients explore how they can excel in today's world where ideas, knowledge and assumptions are readily available and yet can so easily become out-dated. To paraphrase Alvin Toffler, it's easy to feel illiterate in the twenty-first century with the constant pressure to learn, unlearn and relearn.

Learning itself is not difficult – each of us has our own learning style that we use on a daily basis as we read instruction manuals, explore new processes, situations and challenges. The real problem starts when you have to unlearn something first. You can become so fixated on what you already know that it can be hard to let go of the old to let in the new. Every day we are being challenged to unlearn what we thought we knew or how we thought things should be done.

Unlearning is the knowledge battleground of the twenty-first century and those who can do it the most quickly and relearn fastest will lead the way.

Unlearning is the knowledge battleground of the twenty-first century...

97

Put it into action

Strip out the old

Think about unlearning as a way of making space for new, more up-to-date information, like deleting old files on a hard drive, or redecorating your living room where you have to strip away the old wallpaper before you can add a new colour. The problem is, when something's worked for you in the past, there's a tendency to assume that it will keep working for you in the future. This isn't the case. Files get dated and interior design moves on. The most successful people are always happy to question what they know, always open to contradictions and always ready to unlearn.

Unlearn your expectations and assumptions

Avoid preconceived ideas, assumptions and expectations. Don't get fixated on what you expect to happen before doing something new. Change your mindset so that your expectation is to be surprised, challenged, disappointed and forced to start over in your thinking. Be ready to unlearn all of your preconceived ideas. Expectations and assumptions will never prepare you for reality. The experience will always be different from what you expect.

MENTOR OTHERS TO SUCCESS

'Mentoring brings us together – across generation, class, and often race – in a manner that forces us to acknowledge our interdependence, to appreciate, in Martin Luther King, Jr.'s words, that "we are caught in an inescapable network of mutuality, tied to a single garment of destiny".'

Marc Freedman

One of the secrets of success is to constantly help others succeed in *their* goals. In your own life you will have been helped and guided by all kinds of people – parents, grandparents, family friends or teachers, colleagues. Many people might have guided you without even realizing what they were doing – they just talked with you, answered your questions or showed you how to do something. Sometimes just being in someone's presence is enough to teach you something important, such as how to be calm, kind or patient.

Mentoring is an important way to help others and to help yourself at the same time. It can take a number of forms. You might be able to help someone facing similar challenges or life decisions that you have already faced. Perhaps a friend needs help to get through redundancy, divorce or major illness. Or maybe you can help other people see the potential in themselves.

Mentoring is an important way to help others and to help yourself at the same time.

98

Put it into action

Actively seek mentees

The best way to master something is to teach it. If you want learn how to create and have a successful life, then help someone else to learn the same thing. Be ready to give your time and attention to regularly helping others with whatever they have not yet mastered. Sometimes it will be based on your life experiences and common sense – such as helping a friend prepare for a job interview, a relative revise for exams or a colleague to face a marriage crisis. Alternatively, you might find yourself mentoring based on your areas of professional expertise.

Support mentoring of groups

There may be opportunities to mentor people as part of an initiative, for example a reading scheme at a local school or when an HR colleague asks if any staff members are willing to mentor new graduate trainees.

Do not forget your own mentoring

While mentoring others, think about yourself and your needs. How would you benefit from someone's advice and help? Never forget about your own needs or feel embarrassed to ask for support. People rarely say 'no' when asked. Most people love being asked to guide and give advice to others – it makes them feel valued, expert and important.

LEAVE A LEGACY

'I believe our legacy will be defined by the accomplishments and fearless nature by which our daughters and sons take on the global challenges we face.'

Naveen Jain

How do you want to be remembered? Imagine you could listen in on your own funeral. What would you like people to say about you? It's unlikely anyone will have too much to say about your lovely car, house or golf membership. It is your character, behaviour and mindset that people will talk about. It is how you acted towards and treated other people – the qualities you brought to life such as generosity, integrity and kindness. Shakespeare spoke of there being no legacy so rich as honesty and Bill Graham once said that the greatest legacy that we leave our family is not material wealth but our character and faith.

Think about it – how do you remember people who have passed away? I remember a grandfather for the time he always had for me, a grandmother for challenging me to excel, a mother-in-law for her sense that a family should always stay together.

But a legacy isn't only something you leave behind after you die. You leave a legacy whether you intend it or not, at many junctures in your life. Every time you move away from something – a job, workplace, school or neighbourhood – you leave a legacy behind you. Think about these mini-legacies as you move through life and make sure that all your legacies, big and small, are positive for the people left behind.

...make sure that all your legacies, big and small, are positive for the people left behind.

99

Put it into action

Do a 360-degree feedback session

Try asking people – family, friends and colleagues – the following:

- 'How would I be remembered if I were to suddenly disappear?'
- 'What would you think and feel when my name is mentioned?'
- 'What positive and negative ideas or phrases come to mind?'
- 'What impact have I had on you? On how you think, feel and act?'

Calmly listen, smile and thank them for their honest feedback. If you hear something that makes you uncomfortable, do not jump to criticize – just keep calm.

Consciously create legacies

Reflect upon the feedback you have heard. You might be surprised by it and it may make you realize you are far from perfect. Ask yourself what the differing legacies you want to leave in your workplace, your family and broader community are.

Explore the gaps between the legacies you have been creating to date and the legacies you would like to be remembered for.

This gap analysis will give you some areas to work on – it might be focused around behaviours and habits to improve, parts of your personality to nurture or attitudes to change.

If you realize that you have not made a great impression in life so far, don't worry. As long as you are prepared to admit your mistakes, apologize if needed and act differently, you can change people's view of you. You can make them feel loved, valued, listened to and important but it has to be done authentically and sincerely. In the words of Maya Angelou, 'I've learned that people will forget what you said, people will forget what you did, but people will never forget how you made them feel.'

REGRET NOTHING

'...the greatest lesson from his grandfather's life was that he died empty, because he accomplished everything he wanted, with no regrets. I think that, along with leaving a legacy, would be the greatest sign of success.'

Marvin Sapp

Despite the incredible human diversity on the planet, we all have similar regrets when we die. An Australian nurse spent years caring for dying patients and during her conversations with them she explored their biggest regrets. These are the five she heard most often:

1 'I wish I had the courage to live a life true to myself, rather than living the life others expected of me.'

2 'I wish I hadn't worked so hard.'

3 'I wish I hadn't suppressed my own feelings to keep the peace, and instead had the courage to be more honest about what I was feeling.'

4 'I wish I had invested more time in friendships and not lost touch with so many friends over the years.'

5 'I wish I had let myself be happier, smiled more and taken life less seriously.'

Deathbed regrets are an extension of how we live each day. Too often we look back over our shoulders, unhappy with past choices and actions. Your mission to have no regrets at the end of your life starts today.

Your mission to have no regrets at the end of your life starts today.

100

Put it into action

Whom do you need to connect with?

Whom in your life have you failed to express love or gratitude towards? To whom have you caused pain and suffering? Now is the time to connect with them, maybe to apologize for something in the past, to thank them or simply say 'I love you'. If you feel uncertain about this, ask yourself whether the pain and regret of *not* connecting could be greater than the potential pain of reaching out to them.

What do you really want to do?

Is there anything you have been holding back from doing for yourself or for someone else?

I hope this book will have given you the renewed confidence to do these things rather than taking them unfulfilled to your grave. I'd like that to be this book's legacy to you.

AFTERWORD

I spent six months drafting this book followed by another six working with a fantastic team at John Murray Learning, who helped me turn a raw manuscript into the exciting and energizing book you have in your hands today.

During this 12 months of literary toil I came to realize how difficult it is to answer the question 'How do you get to be successful?' in a list of only 100 things. I can now understand Leonardo da Vinci when he said that art is never finished, only abandoned. You might have noticed that some of this book's chapters overlap and that some contain more than just one 'thing' – success, and indeed life, is far too complex to be pigeonholed into 100 discrete boxes. By now I hope you will have learned that your journey to success is about mixing and matching the 100 things and making your own combinations.

As I wrote text, read proofs and talked with my editor, Iain Campbell, I realized that, in addition to the '100 things', I needed to impart to my readers two extra skills or capacities that they would ultimately need to achieve success. I can sum these up as follows:

1 Always be ready to make sacrifices.
2 No matter what happens, life goes on.

Let's look at each of these in turn.

ALWAYS BE READY TO MAKE SACRIFICES

'I think that the good and the great are only separated by the willingness to sacrifice.'

Kareem Abdul-Jabbar

If I were to have a personal motto, it would read, 'Always be ready to make sacrifices', as this reflects what I have faced over the years. However, I only came to truly realize the degree of sacrifice that my life has entailed after I had completed the 12 months spent writing this, my eighth, book. I was so happy that all those evenings and weekends spent toiling away – doing research, reflecting and typing – were finally over. It was only with hindsight that I realized that I had sacrificed so much during this time – turning down invitations to visit friends and attend networking functions as well as missing opportunities to connect with new and existing clients.

In my quest to share with the world my ideas on how to be successful, I had to pay the price in having less time and energy to devote to my coaching and training business ... and, indeed, to helping my teenage son with his homework! Economists have a word for this – opportunity cost. Chasing success in one part of your life may well entail missing out on something else.

What are you willing to sacrifice in your own search for success? It may be useful for you to reflect on this question as you come to the end of this book.

What are you willing to sacrifice in your search for success?

NO MATTER WHAT HAPPENS, LIFE GOES ON

'In three words I can sum up everything I've learned about life: it goes on.'

Robert Frost

During the 12 months that I have spent writing this book, I have experienced many moments of pain, disaster and what might best be described as moments of 'unsuccess'. A few such moments from the last year include:

- One of my son's friends recently died in the middle of his GCSE exams.
- A friend's company, of 15 years' standing and employing a few hundred people, went bankrupt and closed down. My friend now risks losing all his assets and wealth.
- A few of my parents' friends have died, after years of painful illness and incapacity.
- A friend's wife has been diagnosed with late-stage cancer.
- My brother went through a divorce.
- One of my long-standing clients was unexpectedly fired and has spent months fruitlessly hunting for a new job.

You will have experienced such moments yourself or observed those around you going through something similar. It is at moments like these that any plans of achieving goals and dreams can seem a million light years away. Instead, your time will be spent coping with shock, grief, pain, surprise, fear and tears and in supporting others.

But, as Robert Frost so eloquently puts it, life goes on. With time, we can all return to our dreams and goals and continue the path to one form of success or another. What's more, your experience of pain, grief or sadness will mean that you return to your path with a deeper wisdom. Undoubtedly, too, your priorities will have changed – a desire for a peaceful, healthy life may just have supplanted that dream of buying a new sports car!

> With time, we can all return to our dreams and goals and continue the path to one form of success or another.

AND FINALLY...

I would love to hear about your own journey to success. Do connect with me on LinkedIn or on Facebook. I can also be emailed at nigel@silkroadpartnership.com.